Decisive Love

Ron Smith, MD

9 "Therefore know that the LORD your God, He is God, the faithful God who keeps covenant and mercy for a thousand generations with those who love Him and keep His commandments;"

(Deut. 7:9 NKJV)

Copyright © 2024 Ron Smith. V. 2024.0424

All rights reserved. No part of this book may be reproduced in any form or by any electronic or mechanical means, including information storage and retrieval systems, without permission in writing from the publisher, except by reviewers, who may quote brief passages in a review.

Ronnie E. Smith
219 Summer Dr
Morganton, GA 30560

ISBN-13 (hardback): 978-0-9858239-6-2
ISBN-13 (paperback): 978-0-9858239-7-9
ISBN-13 (digital): 978-0-9858239-8-6

Cover art is derived from various works licensed by Dreamstime, https://www.dreamstime.com. (IDs 317491108 & 29586758 ©Melanie Moor, ID 148759504 ©Slaystorm, ID 46385716 ©Steve Fine

Scripture quotations marked ESV are taken from The Holy Bible, English Standard Version®, copyright © 2001 by Crossway, a publishing ministry of Good News Publishers. User by permission. All rights reserved. (Total Verse Count: 238, ESV Word Count/ Total Words: 3019 /11,717 = 25%)

Scripture quotations marked NIV or NIV11 are taken from The Holy Bible, New International Version®, NIV ®. Copyright © 1973, 1978, 1984, 2011 by Biblica, Inc. ® Used by permission of Zondervan. All rights reserved worldwide. www.Zondervan.com. The "NIV" and "New International Version" are trademarks registered in the United States Patent and Trademark Office by Biblica, Inc. ®

Scripture quotations marked NLT or NLT-SE are taken from Holy Bible, New Living Translation, copyright © 1996, 2004, 2007, 2013, 2015 by Tyndale House Foundation. Used by permission of Tyndale House Publishers Inc., Carol Stream, Illinois 60188. All rights reserved.

Scriptures marked AMP are taken from the Amplified® Bible, Copyright © 1954, 1958, 1962, 1964, 1965, 1987 by the Lockman Foundation Used by Permission. www.Lockman.org.

Scriptures marked NAS are taken from the New American Standard Bible®, copyright© 1960, 1962, 1963, 1968, 1971, 1972, 1973, 1975, 1977, 1995 by The Lockman Foundation. Used by permission. www.Lockman.org.

Scripture quotations marked NKJV are taken from the New King James Version®. Copyright © 1982 by Thomas Nelson. Used by permission. All rights reserved.

Scriptures marked KJV are taken from the Holy Bible, King James Version, public domain.

I dedicate this book to my mentors,

Who are also cherished friends,

Tom Langford,

Mike Holman,

&

Larry Shreiner.

Author's Note

Without a doubt, my wife Stacy unknowingly guided the flow of my words onto these pages. Meticulously, she corrected mistakes and improved this book's clarity. Her attention to detail in my writing spilled over from guarding me in all the other ways a wife does.

When we faced almost certain serious medical issues even before Laura was born, Stacy was strong when I was weak. The well-trained physician in me saw Laura's lifelong suffering before it ever began. Courage abandoned me at first, even though I had walked many other sick children through equally tough medical challenges.

Despite a possibly bleak future, the mother in Stacy determined to love our child intensely all the way through to her passing. That strength of heart empowered me through all those hard years when I had to be not only Laura's father, but her physician.

Decisive Love really reflects Stacy's portrait in my words. It tells *our* story of God's work in our lives. I love you, Stacy.

—Ron

Forewords

Ron Smith and I have been friends for several years. Over those years, and, I'm sure long before, Ron has both academically and biblically sought to know who God is, the character of God, and the context of God–how and where God fits into not only creation, human history and time but also our individual lives and experiences. But Ron's search has not been an academic exercise. For him, it has been a spiritual journey. Perhaps to see not only where God has been at work in his life, but more so, to see where he has fit into God's will for his life.

In the first chapter of *Decisive Love*, Ron writes: Jesus never did anything without a good reason. In other words, God has a plan. Through his research of biblical verbiage and the contexts in which and how the words and phrases were used, Ron leads his readers to an understanding of the different types of love. This understanding reveals the ultimate love for us to desire. Whether receiving love or giving love, it is agape love.

Chapter by chapter Ron shows how the different loves, some good, some bad, fail in comparison to agape love, yet how some can lead us to agape love–the love God has for us, and the love we should have for others.

At the end of the book, Ron tells the story of Stacy and his daughter Laura. He talks about Laura's physical challenges, and the trials Stacy and he struggled through. He shares about an abusive caregiver, and Laura's ultimate passing. In this story, Ron doesn't question God's goodness or God's love or God's faithfulness. He lays it at the feet of a sinful world, a world that fails to love one another as Jesus commanded.

From the beginning to the end of *Decisive Love*, Ron Smith has written an excellent book explaining that God loves us because he is love, but we too must be decisive in loving one another. I highly recommend you read this book. It will open your eyes, soften your heart, and move you to love your neighbor.

—Thomas W. Langford, Sr., Retired Pastor, AA, BA, Mdiv, May 13, 2024, Blairsville, Georgia

I've gotten to know Dr. Ron over the last four years, first through men's bible studies but more intimately by sharing coffee on Monday mornings. Little did I know that he was my granddaughter's pediatrician for years in West Georgia. My son and daughter-in-law loved him as their child's doctor. Ron is a loving husband, father, and devoted friend and loves the Lord Jesus. He is committed to seeing people come to know Jesus Christ.

After reading his last book *Between Justice & Mercy*, I was excited to know he was writing the new book, *Decisive Love*. He had taught on it in our men's bible study. The message has had an amazing impact on all our lives, so much I have given him the name, "The Love Doctor. "

In his book, *Decisive Love*, Dr. Ron shares with each of us the only kind of love that really changes lives and relationships. Ron dives deep into the Holy Scriptures to show us the love God has for each of us through his son Jesus, and how we, as his children, show love to others.

As one who is serving as an elder, Sunday school teacher, leading men's Bible studies, and a past missions leader, I would highly recommend this book for those who want to learn and share more about God's decisive love.

—Mike Holman, May 3, 2024, Blairsville, Georgia

As you explore the words of this book, you are also exploring the heart of a man who deeply loves God, and those he has created. To many, Ron is known as "Dr. Love" because of his deep desire to love others as God loves them. For Ron, this is not a casual activity, but a challenge God has placed upon him. A challenge to love others as Jesus has commanded when he said in Luke 10:27, "Love your neighbor as you love yourself."

Decisive Love gives you the opportunity to learn how to develop a love for others that becomes infectious. Not only will this love spread from one to another, it will also draw others into a loving fellowship with you. A fellowship enabling you to understand and meet the needs of those surrounding your life.

Before turning this page, ask the Holy Spirit to prepare your spirit to learn to love others in God's way.

—Larry Schreiner, May 13, 2024, Blairsville, Georgia

Decisive Love

"Do You Love Me?" 1

Friendship Love 5

Family Love 9

Romantic Love 15

Love of Money & Self-Love 21

Decisive Love 33

Forgiveness 45

Prayer 55

Final Thoughts 61

Appendix & Supplementals

    Laura's Story 65

    Bookmark Timeline Reference 71

    Our Spiritual Anatomy 79

    Guide To Kohlenberger/Mounce Hebrew-Aramaic Dictionary ... 91

    Bibliography & Endnotes 95

CHAPTER ONE

"Do You Love Me?"

Like most other Christians, I had always been a little puzzled by this conversation between Jesus and Simon Peter. Three times after his resurrection, Jesus asked him, "Do you love me?" Three times, Peter answered yes. Jesus *never* did anything without a good reason, but I could not at first see the point of this conversation.

> 15 When they had finished breakfast, Jesus said to Simon Peter, "Simon, son of John, do you *love* {*agapaō*} me more than these?" He said to him, "Yes, Lord; you know that I *love* {*phileō*} you." He said to him, "Feed my lambs." 16 He said to him a second time, "Simon, son of John, do you *love* {*agapaō*} me?" He said to him, "Yes, Lord; you know that I *love* {*phileō*} you." He said to him, "Tend my sheep." 17 He said to him the third time, "Simon, son of John, do you *love* {*phileō*} me?" Peter was grieved because he said to him the third time, "Do you *love* {*phileō*} me?" and he said to him, "Lord, you know everything; you

know that I *love* {***phileō***} you." Jesus said to him, "Feed my sheep." (John 21:15–17 ESV)

Why did Peter use *phileō*, which means love between friends when Jesus is asking if he loves him unconditionally? He is surely not oblivious when Jesus says *agapaō* twice in a row before finally using *phileō*. The *Scofield® Study Bible Notes*[1] entertains the thought that because this conversation occurred after the resurrection, Peter used the lesser and "safer" *phileō* over *agapaō* out of shame. While that may be partly true, in Galatians, Paul rebukes Peter for acting differently towards the Gentiles in the presence of fellow Jews.

The context emerges when you look at each original word translated as "love." In the first two instances, Jesus uses the Greek word *agapaō* (ag-ap-ah´-o). Peter responds each time with *phileō* (fil-eh´-o). On his third try, Jesus concedes to him using *phileō* instead of *agapaō*. One can see how the richer, original Greek in all three cases loses context in the English translation. It left me wondering what Jesus was actually trying to say.

Loss of context in translation is not unique to Greek. The Hebrew in Exodus uses two different words for "love" which have meanings analogous to *agapaō* and *phileō*. In the verses below, notice the phrase "steadfast love" and "those who love me." The Hebrew word for love translated from "steadfast love" is *ḥesed* (kheh´-sed). In Strong's Hebrew Concordance, it means loving-kindness and mercy, and is the Hebrew analogue of the Greek word *agapaō*. The word love, in the translated phrase "those who love me," comes from the Hebrew word *ʾāhaḇ* (aw-hab´), which refers in particular to the affection of a friend or family member. *Agapaō* and *ḥesed* are talking about the same unconditional love of God.

There is no point faulting Peter, because we too don't naturally understand God's *agapaō* love. The Holy Spirit has to reveal God's unconditional love to our heart. The terms "saved" or "unsaved" simply mean we responded and accepted his love or drew back in refusal. The only unforgivable sin is refusing his powerful and decisive *agapaō* love.

In the chapters that follow, you are going to learn about the six loves. C.S. Lewis inspired me with his description of the four loves. The other two are important in understanding decisive love.

CHAPTER TWO

Friendship Love

I related in the previous chapter how Peter responded to the question, "...do you love me..." with the Greek word *phileō* instead of *agapaō*, which Jesus used. After asking the question twice, Jesus finally himself uses *phileō*. Let's not analyze this interaction to see why Jesus conceded to Peter's word. Rather, let's look a little harder at the original words in Scripture for and about friendship love. According to Mounce's Greek dictionary, *phileō* translates in the following ways.

> **GK G5797 | S G5368 φιλέω** *phileō* (fil-eh´-o) 25x
> pr. to manifest some act or token of kindness or affection; to kiss, Mt. 26:48; Mk. 14:44; Lk. 22:47; to love, regard with affection, have affection for, Mt. 10:37; Jn. 5:20; to like, be fond of, delight in a thing, Mt. 23:6; Rev. 22:15; to cherish inordinately, set store by, Jn. 12:25 » love.[1]

Searching the Old and New Testament for "friend," "friendship," and "neighbor" expands the scope of friendship love.

GK H8276 | S H7453 רֵעַ *rēaʿ* (ray´-ah) 188x n.m. [8287]. neighbor; friend, companion, associate. » friend; neighbor; other.[2]

GK H170 | S H157 אָהַב *ʾāhab* (aw-hab´) 217x v. [root of: 171, 172, 173, 174?, 175]. **Q** to love, like, be a friend; **N** to be loved; **P** be a lover, an ally; love can refer to friendship, familial love, romantic love, or covenant loyalty. » like; love.[3]

GK G2279 | S G2083 ἑταῖρος *hetairos* (het-ah´-ee-ros) 3x a companion, associate, fellow-comrade, friend, Mt. 20:13; 22:12; 26:50 •[4]

GK G5813 | S G5384 φίλος *philos* (fee´-los) 29x loved, dear; devoted; Acts 19:31; as a subst., a friend, Lk. 7:6; 11:5, 6, 8; a congenial associate, Mt. 11:19; Lk. 7:34; Jas. 4:4; used as a word of courteous appellation, Lk. 14:10 » friend.[5]

GK G4446 | S G4139 πλησίον *plēsion* (play-see´-on) 17x can function as an improper prep., near, near by, Jn. 4:5; ὁ πλησίον, a neighbor, Mt. 19:19; Rom. 15:2; a friendly neighbor, Mt. 5:43 » near; neighbor.[6]

Who then is our friend? Maybe the better question is who *should* be our friend? For a Bible study session I taught at my local church's men's Bible study, I coined the phrase "Don't Be FFF!" I chuckled when one of my good friends there immediately came up empty-handed in his web search because I had just originated the phrase. It stands for "Don't Be Fooled by the Facade of Form."

Everything we experience through sight, smell, touch, sound, or odor presents a form. Good-looking cars, people, sports, politicians as well as scoundrels, criminals, and terrorists project form whether good or bad. We respond based on surface qualities which really tell us nothing about the quality, character, or true desirability beneath. Beauty is skin deep and can cover a rotten core.

Lust of the eyes and flesh, and the pride of life result from a surface facade. This begins with how we view and treat strangers. We may hesitate to extend true loving friendship in order to protect ourselves or an established clique of friends. An immaculately groomed and handsome man or beautiful woman presents a pitfall equal to an unkempt, homeless, dirty, smelly beggar. Have you ever fawned over the attractive or withdrawn from the repulsive? Was Jesus ever fooled by the facade of anyone's appearance?

His blood-stained new covenant required obedience to only two inseparable commands. Jesus told us to love God with all our heart despite all. Because God loves each of us, his first command *requires* us to love our neighbors the same way. "Love" in those verses translates from unconditional *agapaō* love, which is not the same as friendship love. But friendship love opens our heart and plants agape love so we can love people most deeply.

Every person I meet, I try really hard to remember their name. I push my embarrassment back when I awkwardly forget. Sidestepping self-consciousness, I beg forgiveness and ask them to tell me again. I do this until I know them because names carry significance. Revelation 2:12 and 3:17 says he will give us a new name, and throughout Scripture it says that we will know God by his name. Friendship love begins when you know a person's name.

It takes effort to show friendship love. I don't cook much, but I make a pretty delicious cheddar biscuit. In order to get to know my neighbors, I started giving them fresh, hot batches made just for them. Cooking is an effort for me, and this gift speaks louder than my words. In all my friendship circles, I relate to each person individually. What is important to them becomes important to me.

Deep agape love for neighbors, strangers, and fellow church members begins with learning and using their names. I have recorded names on my phone and have often visited our directory app to help me. The biggest hurdle is fear. Overcoming our internal fear of "putting ourselves out there" leads us to use a person's name at the end of "I love you."

Extending friendship love allows us to next extend unconditional agape love to people. This pleases our Father.

CHAPTER THREE

Family Love

The Greek word *storge* (στοργη, stor´-gee) is not in Scripture, however *astorgos* is found twice. *Storge* means natural, familial love between parents and children, so *astorgos* means the absence of that affection. It is translated "heartless" in Romans and 2 Timothy. In the Old Testament, the Hebrew word *ʾāhab* can also mean familial love just as it can be used for other kinds of love. Proverbs 17:17 associates its friendship meaning with that of brotherly affection.

> **GK G845 | S G794** ἄστοργος *astorgos* (as´-tor-gos) 2x devoid of natural or instinctive affection, without affection to kindred, Rom. 1:31; 2 Tim. 3:3*[1]
>
> **GK H170 | S H157** אָהַב *ʾāhab* (aw-habe´) 217x v. [root of: 171, 172, 173, 174?, 175]. **Q** to love, like, be a friend; **N** to be loved; **P** be a lover, an ally; love can refer to friendship, familial love, romantic love, or covenant loyalty. » like; love.[2]

28 And since they did not see fit to acknowledge God, God gave them up to a debased mind to do what

ought not to be done. ²⁹ They were filled with all manner of unrighteousness, evil, covetousness, malice. They are full of envy, murder, strife, deceit, maliciousness. They are gossips, ³⁰ slanderers, haters of God, insolent, haughty, boastful, inventors of evil, disobedient to parents, ³¹ foolish, faithless, *heartless {astorgos}*, ruthless. ³² Though they know God's righteous decree that those who practice such things deserve to die, they not only do them but give approval to those who practice them. (Rom. 1:28-32 ESVS)

¹ But understand this, that in the last days there will come times of difficulty. ² For people will be lovers of self, lovers of money, proud, arrogant, abusive, disobedient to their parents, ungrateful, unholy, ³ *heartless {astorgos}*, unappeasable, slanderous, without self-control, brutal, not loving good, ⁴ treacherous, reckless, swollen with conceit, lovers of pleasure rather than lovers of God, ⁵ having the appearance of godliness, but denying its power. (2Tim. 3:1-5 ESVS)

¹⁷ A friend *loves {ʾāhab}* at all times,
    and a brother is born for adversity.
(Prov. 17:17 ESVS)

I'm well into my 60s, and the significance of family love long since hit home. Friends at church often tell me of their broken or dysfunctional parent-child relationships and strained, warped, or non-existent sibling bonds. How will any family survive intact in these last days?

The very first broken family occurred when Cain killed Abel. We don't know how Adam and Eve reacted, but it must have been horrible. Cain left his family and fled east of Eden to Nod, and 1 John 3:12 declares he was of the evil one. Sin means any behavior contrary to n and in rebellion against our Father's character. There is no such thing as a "small" sin or degrees of separation from God. Either you abide with him or you do not.

The story of the prodigal son tells us there is hope. Proverbs 22:6 tells parents to bring up their children in righteousness, but it also says they can return many years after rejecting that upbringing. Ephesians 6:4 commands us not to provoke our children to anger. How many times has my own pride provoked my daughter to anger instead of lovingly and patiently instructing as I should have done! Did Adam or Eve provoke Cain? Even when parents do everything right, each child makes their own choices. All these possibilities tell us something every mother or father learns. Parenting is hard.

Titus 2:2-6 gives very specific instructions for fathers and mothers. These verses use the English word "love," however, it is translated from the Greek word *agapē*. Obviously, family love has a strong Scriptural connection to God's kind of covenant love. The other significant Greek word *hypomonē* translates to steadfastness, which is a key aspect of covenant love.

> **GK G27 | S G26** ἀγάπη *agapē* (ag-ah´-pay) 116x love, generosity, kindly concern, devotedness; pl. love-feasts, Jude 12 » love.[3]

GK G5705 | S G5281 ὑπομονή *hypomonē* (hoop-om-on-ay´) 32x patient endurance, 2 Cor. 12:12; Col. 1:11; patient awaiting, Lk. 21:19; a patient frame of mind, patience, Rom. 5:3, 4; 15:4, 5; Jas. 1:3; perseverance, Rom. 2:7; endurance in adherence to an object, 1 Thess. 1:3; 2 Thess. 3:5; Rev. 1:9; ἐν ὑπομονῇ and δι' ὑπομονῆς, constantly, perseveringly, Lk. 8:15; Rom. 8:25; Heb. 12:1; an enduring of affliction, etc., the act of suffering, undergoing, etc., 2 Cor. 1:6; 6:4 » endurance, endure; perseverance.[4]

GK G5405 | S G4994 σωφρονίζω *sōphronizō* (so-fron-id´-zo) 1x encourage, to restore to a right mind; to make sober-minded, to steady by exhortation and guidance, Tit. 2:4*[5]

2 Older men are to be sober-minded, dignified, self-controlled, sound in faith, in *love {agapē}*, and in *steadfastness {hypomonē}*. 3 Older women likewise are to be reverent in behavior, not slanderers or slaves to much wine. They are to teach what is good, 4 and so train the young women to *love {sōphronizō}* their husbands and children, 5 to be self-controlled, pure, working at home, kind, and submissive to their own husbands, that the word of God may not be reviled. 6 Likewise, urge the younger men to be self-controlled. (Titus 2:2-6 ESVS)

The story of the prodigal son in Luke 15:11-32 is the best example of family love based in unconditional *agapē* love. Not only did the father love his son as a child, he loved him unconditionally. He didn't try to entice the boy to remain at home by loving him as a friend instead of a father. He loved him so much he was willing to let him walk away. When his son returned, he didn't love him less.

A child's disrespectful, demeaning, or demanding ways challenge parent's efforts to love them as God loves them. Bargaining down parental love to a friendship breeds rebelliousness. Children need us to be parents and not friends. It injures them further and breeds more rebellion.

It is no accident that we call God our Father. We are his children and together a family. When he finally makes us just like Jesus, all rebellion and broken relationships will end. Our families here are a shadow of his family in heaven.

Satan targets families specifically to attack foundational *agapē* love. Destroying family love can also kill romantic and friendship love, as well as steadfast love for God.

CHAPTER FOUR

Romantic Love

Eros (ερως *é-rōs*) can refer to the Greek god or to passionate, sensual love. The debased word "erotica" comes from it. While not directly found in Scripture, the Hebrew word *ʾāhaḇ* and the Greek *agapaō* encompasses true romantic love. The Song of Solomon reveals true romantic love between a man and woman. Notice the words *ʾahaḇāh raʿyāh* translated as "my love" in the Song of Solomon below.

> **GK H170 | S H157** אָהַב *ʾāhaḇ* (aw-hab´) 217x v. [root of: 171, 172, 173, 174?, 175]. **Q** to love, like, be a friend; **N** to be loved; **P** be a lover, an ally; love can refer to friendship, familial love, romantic love, or covenant loyalty. » like; love.[1]
>
> **GK H173 | S H160** אַהֲבָה *ʾahaḇāh* (a-hab-aw) 33x n.f. [170]. love; friendship, familial love, romantic love, or covenant loyalty.[2]
>
> **GK H8299 | S H7474** רַעְיָה *raʿyāh* (rah-yaw´) 9x n.f. [8287]. darling, beloved, formally, companion, a woman who is the object of a man's love and affection.[3]

Romantic Love

GK G26 | S G25 ἀγαπάω *agapaō* (ag-ap-ah´-o) 143x to love, value, esteem, feel or manifest generous concern for, be faithful towards; to delight in, to set store upon, Rev. 12:11 » love.⁴

⁸ I charge you, O daughters of Jerusalem, if ye find my beloved, that ye tell him, that I am sick of *love* {*ʾahaḇāh*}. (Song 5:8 KJVS)

⁴ ¶ Thou art beautiful, O my *love* {*raʿyāh*}, as Tirzah, comely as Jerusalem, terrible as an army with banners. (Song 6:4 KJVS)

If you didn't understand what the original words meant, you might think the Song of Solomon is really about erotica. True Scriptural romantic love succumbed long ago to cinematic, sensual erotica. Don't be fooled by the facade of erotic form! Pornography kills every aspect of romance.

True Scriptural romantic love originates in the ancient Jewish wedding ceremony for which even most Jews today have little knowledge. Their wedding traditions carry some of its symbols, but the original meaning seems lost. Historically, it comprised three parts called the *shiddukhin*, *erusin*, and *nissuin*. Though a woman's father represented her, the marriage was not truly arranged. The potential groom, or his representative father, approached the woman's father with a marriage offer. The prospective bride's father then discussed the proposal with his daughter who made the decision to accept or reject a marriage. Genesis 24 reveals how Rebekah made the ultimate decision to accept the marriage. They were not married until she arrived in Canaan.

The shiddukhin began when the bride accepted the offer of marriage. Her father and bridegroom negotiated the *mohar* or bride price, which would offset her family's economic loss. The bride price could be very costly. Recall Jacob paid in total for Leah and Rachel with fourteen years of hard labor.

Once they agreed on the mohar, the bride and groom performed a ceremonial water cleansing signifying the event's solemness. The *ketubah* marriage document specified not only the mohar but also what the bride was to receive should the groom divorce her. With their signatures, they were legally married, and never betrothed or engaged. The shiddukhin was complete.

One ketubah copy went to each of their parents and another as a legal record to the local synagogue. Though legally married, bride and bridegroom went back father's homes without consummating. The groom began adding their room onto his father's house while his new bride patiently waited for the *erusin*.

Mary became pregnant with Jesus when she and Joseph were at this point in their marriage. The waiting period could last from one to seven years. It demonstrated a new wife's purity because any infidelity resulting in pregnancy would be exposed. Joseph had every legal right to stone Mary because she was clearly pregnant.

Romantic Love

The wait ended when the bridegroom's father commanded his son to go get his bride. Arriving at her house, the groom paid to her father, the mohar. The erusin began when he and his bride consummated in the *chuppah* chamber. Spread beneath her lay the white chuppah cloth. As they entered the room, their witnesses waited outside the chamber door listening. At the sight of her fresh blood on the chuppah cloth, the bridegroom began whooping joyfully. Those outside the chuppah chamber immediately joined in his joyous shouting. Her fresh blood was proof of her purity.

Her parents kept the chuppah cloth as legal proof of their daughter's purity. Bride in hand, they departed for his father's house for the nissuin wedding feast, never to be separated. The mohar for us, the church, was Jesus's own body. The chuppah cloth blood was his, and the justified purity, ours. Presently, he is in heaven preparing our new home and giving everyone time to hear and accept his bride price and blood. Daily his bride, the church grows. She stands ready for his instant call to the nissuin wedding feast.

The evening of 14 Nissan is the day before Passover and is called the Day of Preparation of Passover in Scripture. We call it the Last Supper, but it was not a Passover meal since there was no roasted sacrificial lamb anywhere. The bread Jesus breaks represents the bride price, which is his body, and the wine his own blood which would make his bride, the church, pure. Jesus died with all the other Passover lambs hours before dusk ushered in Passover on 15 Nisan. His words about eating his flesh and drinking his blood now make sense in light of ancient Jewish wedding ceremony. At the time of Jesus's death, people knew and understood this wedding tradition. They missed the one who came to save them from their sinful nature because they were expecting a great military messiah.

> 52 The Jews then disputed among themselves, saying, "How can this man give us his flesh to eat?" 53 So Jesus said to them, "Truly, truly, I say to you, unless you eat the flesh of the Son of Man and drink his blood, you have no life in you. 54 Whoever feeds on my flesh and drinks my blood has eternal life, and I will raise him up on the last day. 55 For my flesh is true food, and my blood is true drink. 56 Whoever feeds on my flesh and drinks my blood abides in me, and I in him." (John 6:52-56 ESVS)

The greater significance of changing water to wine at Cana cannot be understated. Jesus's first public miracle was the clue his relationship with us would be that of a bride and groom. John didn't baptize Jesus in the Jordan because he needed to repent. All John's baptisms, including that of Jesus, were to prepare the way for the ceremonial cleansing for the ketubah marriage document. Even though Jesus long since paid the bride price and provided our chuppah cloth purity at the cross, baptism today symbolizes the ceremonial inclusion of new believers in the ketubah covenant.

With his crucifixion and resurrection complete, the erusin if finished. Jesus is presently preparing all the rooms in his Father's house to receive us. We wait only for the trumpet blast beckoning us to come home and sit at God's great nissuin wedding feast. Jesus's last words assure all that day is coming. He loves his bride, the church, and we believers will someday be with him forever.

> ¹ "Let not your hearts be troubled. Believe in God; believe also in me. ² In my Father's house are many rooms. If it were not so, would I have told you that I go to prepare a place for you? ³ And if I go and prepare a place for you, I will come again and will take you to myself, that where I am you may be also." (John 14:1-3 ESVS)

> ⁷ Let us rejoice and exult
>   and give him the glory,
> for the *marriage* {*gamos*} of the Lamb has come,
>   and his *Bride* {*gynē*} has made herself ready;
> (Rev. 19:7 ESVS)

GK G1141 | S G1062 γάμος *gamos* {gam´-os} 16x a wedding; nuptial festivities, a marriage festival, Mt. 22:2; 25:10; Jn. 2:1, 2; Rev. 19:7, 9; any feast or banquet, Lk. 12:36; 14:8; the marriage state, Heb. 13:4 » marry, marriage; wedding.[5]

GK G1222 | S G1135 γυνή *gynē* {goo-nay´} 215x a woman, Mt. 5:28, et al.; a married woman, wife, Mt. 5:31, 32; 14:3, et al.; in the voc. w° gu/nai, O woman! an ordinary mode of addressing females under every circumstance; met. used of the Church, as united to Christ, Rev. 19:7; 21:9 » wife; woman.[6]

CHAPTER FIVE

Love of Money & Self-Love

While friendship, family, and romantic love have good yet corruptible aspects, two other "loves" always destroy. *Philargyros,* or the love of money, is also the love of wealth, riches, and power. *Aphilargyros* is the absence of the love of money. Four verses from Luke, Hebrews, and two from Timothy explain our relationship with mammon.

> **GK G5795 | S G5366** φιλάργυρος *philargyros* (fil-ar´-goo-ros) 2x money-loving, covetous, Lk. 16:14; 2 Tim. 3:2*[1]
>
> **GK G921 | S G866** ἀφιλάργυρος *aphilargyros* (af-il-ar´-goo-ros) 2x not fond of money, not covetous, generous, 1 Tim. 3:3; Heb. 13:5*[2]

[1] He also said to the disciples, "There was a rich man who had a manager, and charges were brought to him that this man was wasting his possessions. [2] And he called him and said to him, 'What is this that I hear about you? Turn in the account of your management, for you can no longer be manager.' [3] And the manager said to himself, 'What shall I do, since my master is

taking the management away from me? I am not strong enough to dig, and I am ashamed to beg. 4 I have decided what to do, so that when I am removed from management, people may receive me into their houses.' 5 So, summoning his master's debtors one by one, he said to the first, 'How much do you owe my master?' 6 He said, 'A hundred measures of oil.' He said to him, 'Take your bill, and sit down quickly and write fifty.' 7 Then he said to another, 'And how much do you owe?' He said, 'A hundred measures of wheat.' He said to him, 'Take your bill, and write eighty.' 8 The master commended the dishonest manager for his shrewdness. For the sons of this world are more shrewd in dealing with their own generation than the sons of light. 9 And I tell you, make friends for yourselves by means of unrighteous wealth, so that when it fails they may receive you into the eternal dwellings."

10 "One who is faithful in a very little is also faithful in much, and one who is dishonest in a very little is also dishonest in much. 11 If then you have not been faithful in the unrighteous wealth, who will entrust to you the true riches? 12 And if you have not been faithful in that which is another's, who will give you that which is your own? 13 No servant can serve two masters, for either he will hate the one and love the other, or he will be devoted to the one and despise the other. You cannot serve God and money."

14 The Pharisees, who were *lovers of money* {*philargyros*}, heard all these things, and they ridiculed him. 15 And he said to them, "You are those who

justify yourselves before men, but God knows your hearts. For what is exalted among men is an abomination in the sight of God. 16 The Law and the Prophets were until John; since then the good news of the kingdom of God is preached, and everyone forces his way into it. 17 But it is easier for heaven and earth to pass away than for one dot of the Law to become void." (Luke 16:1-17 ESVS)

1 The saying is trustworthy: If anyone aspires to the office of overseer, he desires a noble task. 2 Therefore an overseer must be above reproach, the husband of one wife, sober-minded, self-controlled, respectable, hospitable, able to teach, 3 not a drunkard, not violent but gentle, not quarrelsome, *not a lover of money* {*aphilargyros*}. (1Tim. 3:1 ESVS)

5 Keep your life *free from love of money* {*aphilargyros*}, and be content with what you have, for he has said, "I will never leave you nor forsake you." (Heb. 13:5 ESVS)

The deceit of the power, wealth, and riches did not just affect religious leaders. A rich man approached Jesus, asking what he needed to do to inherit eternal life. He walked away dejected because he would not part with his riches. Jesus remarked it was easier for a rich man to go through the eye of a needle than to enter heaven. Some say it was not the eye of a sewing needle, but an inner gate in a city wall where a camel could pass only if stooped and unloaded. Either way, the rich man loved his riches and left without being saved.

Philautos is not respect for one's self, body, or being but rather narcissistic self-absorption that fully corrupts. The Greek word *philautos* only occurs once in the New Testament, where it is an epidemic sign of the last days. Self-love allows no room to love anyone, and Timothy associates it with *aphilargyros*, which is translated "heartless."

> **GK G5796 | S G5367 φίλαυτος** *philautos* {fil´-ow-tos} 1x self-loving; selfish, 2 Tim. 3:2*[3]

> [1] But understand this, that in the last days there will come times of difficulty. [2] For people will be *lovers of self {philautos}, lovers of money {philargyros}*, proud, arrogant, abusive, disobedient to their parents, ungrateful, unholy, [3] *heartless {aphilargyros}*, unappeasable, slanderous, without self-control, brutal, not loving good, [4] treacherous, reckless, swollen with conceit, lovers of pleasure rather than lovers of God, [5] having the appearance of godliness, but denying its power. (2Tim. 3:1 ESVS)

The combination of *philautos* and *philargyros* destroyed Satan's beauty and place of authority. No doubt his self-adoration brought a third of angels down as described in Revelation 12. Ezekiel and Isaiah graphically account how he crashed to the ground, completely blackened and burnt. Hatred and thirst for revenge against God and power still saturates and motivates him despite knowing his eventual destruction.

> [11] Moreover, the word of the LORD came to me:
> [12] "Son of man, raise a lamentation over the king of
>   Tyre, and say to him, Thus says the Lord GOD:

"You were the signet of perfection,
  full of wisdom and perfect in beauty.
13 You were in Eden, the garden of God;
   every precious stone was your covering,
  sardius, topaz, and diamond,
   beryl, onyx, and jasper,
  sapphire, emerald, and carbuncle;
   and crafted in gold were your settings
    and your engravings.
  On the day that you were created
   they were prepared.
14 You were an anointed guardian cherub.
   I placed you; you were on the holy mountain
    of God;
   in the midst of the stones of fire you walked.
15 You were blameless in your ways
   from the day you were created,
    till unrighteousness was found in you.
16 In the abundance of your trade
   you were filled with violence in your midst, and
    you sinned;
  so I cast you as a profane thing from the mountain
   of God,
   and I destroyed you, O guardian cherub,
    from the midst of the stones of fire.
17 Your heart was proud because of your beauty;
   you corrupted your wisdom for the sake of your
    splendor.
  I cast you to the ground;
   I exposed you before kings,
    to feast their eyes on you.
18 By the multitude of your iniquities,
   in the unrighteousness of your trade

  you profaned your sanctuaries;
 so I brought fire out from your midst;
  it consumed you,
 and I turned you to ashes on the earth
  in the sight of all who saw you.
19 All who know you among the peoples
  are appalled at you;
 you have come to a dreadful end
  and shall be no more forever."
(Ezek. 28:11-19 ESVS)

12 "How you are fallen from heaven,
  O Day Star, son of Dawn!
 How you are cut down to the ground,
  you who laid the nations low!
13 You said in your heart,
  'I will ascend to heaven;
 above the stars of God
  I will set my throne on high;
 I will sit on the mount of assembly
  in the far reaches of the north;
14 I will ascend above the heights of the clouds;
  I will make myself like the Most High.'
15 But you are brought down to Sheol,
  to the far reaches of the pit.
16 Those who see you will stare at you
  and ponder over you:
 'Is this the man who made the earth tremble,
  who shook kingdoms,
17 who made the world like a desert
  and overthrew its cities,
   who did not let his prisoners go home?'
18 All the kings of the nations lie in glory,

> each in his own tomb;
> 19 but you are cast out, away from your grave,
>   like a loathed branch,
>   clothed with the slain, those pierced by the sword,
>   who go down to the stones of the pit,
>   like a dead body trampled underfoot.
> 20 You will not be joined with them in burial,
>   because you have destroyed your land,
>   you have slain your people.
>   "May the offspring of evildoers
>   nevermore be named!
> 21 Prepare slaughter for his sons
>   because of the guilt of their fathers,
>   lest they rise and possess the earth,
>   and fill the face of the world with cities."
> (Is. 14:12-21 ESVS)

CHAPTER SIX

The Context of God

We all experience friendship, family, and romantic love through the stream of time. Even the love of money and self-love flows this way. Somehow, we forget our time-bound experience does not apply at all to God. His context is different.

> "In the last chapter I had to touch on the subject of prayer, and while that is still fresh in your mind and my own, I should like to deal with a difficulty that some people find about the whole idea of prayer. A man put it to me by saying 'I can believe in God all right, but what I cannot swallow is the idea of Him attending to several hundred million human beings who are all addressing Him at the same moment.' And I have found that quite a lot of people feel this.
>
> Now, the first thing to notice is that the whole sting of it comes in the words at the same moment. Most of us can imagine God attending to any number of applicants if only they came one by one and He had an endless time to do it in. So what is really at the back of this difficulty is the idea of God having to fit too many things into one moment of time."
> -C. S. Lewis[1]

Following my daughter's death in 2012, I plunged into a deep place. How important those two paragraphs became after I listened to the *Mere Christianity* audiobook several hundred times. Most people think God experiences life with us moment by moment. The fact is, he exists outside our stream of time. God knows already what you will pray, say, and do tomorrow as well as how he will answer. He knew my grief before I did, and he knew what I needed to carry me through it.

God's central character of love existed in timelessness before creation. The boundary of his sovereign authority began *with* creation. He thought of you before creation. He already knew everything you would do, say, or think before you were a single cell in your mother's womb. This knowing does not mean God predestines our choices or ultimate fate because it would violate his central nature of love. He cannot be tyrant and loving Father simultaneously any more than light can ever be darkness.

Until Albert Einstein's Special Theory of Relativity in 1905, everyone thought time was the same everywhere in the universe. It is not the same. His theory proposed two objects traveling at different speeds experienced the passage of time differently. If one of twin brothers travels in a spaceship flying to and from a far distant galaxy at very near the speed of light, time slows down for him as you can see in Table 2. The difference can be calculated using the Time Dilation Equation which came out of Einstein's theory.[2]

Time Dilation

$$t' = t\sqrt{1 - \frac{v^2}{c^2}}$$

t' :: time for astronaunt
t :: time for brother
v :: astronaut velocity
c :: speed of light (or 1)

Astronaut Traveling This Percent of c *	Astronaut's Lapsed Time	Brother's Lapsed Time
50%	8.6 years	10 years
75%	6.6 years	10 years
90%	4.4 years	10 years
99%	1.4 years	10 years
99.999 9%	5 days	10 years
99.999 999%	1.2 hours	10 years
99.999 999 999 99%	44.5 seconds	10 years
99.999 999 999 999 999 99%	0.004 seconds	10 years
100%	no time	all amounts of time

*The speed of light c is 186,246 miles per second or 299,792,458 meters per second.

Table 2. The Relative Effect of Speed on the Passage of Time

Timelessness is mathematically real. Sunlight leaves the sun and arrives at the surface of the Earth in about eight and a half minutes. While we are waiting for the sunlight to arrive, that light experiences no passage of time at all instantly from its frame of reference traversing the ninety million miles from the Sun to the Earth.

Scripture says God is light, and this is not just philosophical mumbo jumbo. Scripture also declares God exists in a timeless realm. How many times have you heard or read this verse from 2 Peter? My calculations show exquisite mathematically accuracy!

> [8] But do not overlook this one fact, beloved, that with the Lord one day is as a thousand years, and a thousand years as one day. (2Pet. 3:8 ESVS)

One Day with God Equals 1000 Years

```
; Using the Time Dilation Equation
; where c_frac is the fraction
; of c, the speed of light
; i.e., c_frac = a fraction of c,
; and from 2 Peter 3:8, t' is one day
; t is 1000 years or 365,256.36 days
```

$$t' = t\sqrt{1 - c_{frac}}$$

$$\begin{aligned} c_{frac} &= 1 - \left(\frac{t'}{t}\right)^2 \\ &= 1 - \left(\frac{1 \text{ day}}{365{,}256.36 \text{ days}}\right)^2 \\ &= 0.999999999992 \end{aligned}$$

```
; so
```

$$c_{frac} = 0.999999999992 \times c$$
$$c_{frac} \simeq c \ (i.e., \textbf{the speed of light})$$

```
; This means 2 Peter 3:8 is the
; textual equivalent of Einstein's
; Special Theory of Relativity,
; and is mathematically precise!
```

CHAPTER SEVEN

Decisive Love

The New Testament Greek word *agapē* or *agapaō* refers to God's kind of love. Those familiar with it understand it as "unconditional love." The Old Testament Hebrew word *ḥesed* translated "steadfast love" means the same thing. Though they overlap remarkably with friendship, family, and romantic love, steadfast love carries a much greater breadth and intensity. God's unconditional love for us is faithful, covenant love which never changes or falters even if we don't return it or respond to it. This kind of love makes him holy.

> **GK H2876 | S H2617** חֶסֶד *ḥesed* (kheh´-sed) 249x n.m. [root of: 1213, 2877, 2878?, 2883; cf. 2874]. unfailing love, loyal love, devotion, kindness, often based on a prior relationship, especially a covenant relationship. » kindness; love; loyalty; mercy.[1]
>
> **GK G26 | S G25** ἀγαπάω *agapaō* (ag-ap-ah´-o) 143x to love, value, esteem, feel or manifest generous concern for, be faithful towards; to delight in, to set store upon, Rev. 12:11 » love.[2]

Decisive Love

GK G27 | S G26 ἀγάπη *agapē* (ag-ah´-pay) 116x love, generosity, kindly concern, devotedness; pl. love-feasts, Jude 12 » love.³

GK H170 | S H157 אָהֵב *ʾāhaḇ* (aw-hab´) 217x v. [root of: 171, 172, 173, 174?, 175]. **Q** to love, like, be a friend; **N** to be loved; **P** be a lover, an ally; love can refer to friendship, familial love, romantic love, or covenant loyalty. » like; love.⁴

²⁷ and said, "Blessed be the LORD, the God of my master Abraham, who has not forsaken his *steadfast love* {*ḥesed*} and his faithfulness toward my master. As for me, the LORD has led me in the way to the house of my master's kinsmen." (Gen. 24:27 ESVS)

³⁴ You shall treat the stranger who sojourns with you as the native among you, and you shall *love* {*ʾāhaḇ*} him as yourself, for you were strangers in the land of Egypt: I am the LORD your God. (Lev. 19:34 ESVS)

⁹ Know therefore that the LORD your God is God, the faithful God who keeps covenant and *steadfast love* {*ḥesed*} with those who *love* {*ʾāhaḇ*} him and keep his commandments, to a thousand generations, (Deut. 7:9 ESVS)

C. S. Lewis's Law of Human Nature refers to our God-breathed copy of right and wrong. This conscience even gives men the ability to do what is right, having never heard God's law. When they follow their conscience, they become a law unto themselves, and his righteousness is written on their hearts.

> 13 (For not the hearers of the law are just before God, but the doers of the law shall be justified. 14 For when the Gentiles, which have not the law, do by nature the things contained in the law, these, having not the law, are a law unto themselves: 15 Which shew the work of the law written in their hearts, their conscience also bearing witness, and their thoughts the mean while accusing or else excusing one another;) (Rom. 2:13-15 KJVS)

When God breathed life and conscience into us, he also infused the ability to give and receive friendship, family, and romantic loves. Just as our conscience is a copy of his righteousness, these natural loves are derivative copies of God's covenant love. Psalm and Isaiah declare he sends out his love which, like his word, will not return void.

> 3 He will send from heaven and save me;
>   he will put to shame him who tramples on me.
>   *Selah*
>   God will *send* out his *steadfast love* and
>   his faithfulness!
> (Psa. 57:3 ESVS)

> 11 so shall my word be that *goes out from my mouth*;
>   it shall not return to me empty,
>   but it shall accomplish that which I purpose,
>   and shall succeed in the thing for which I *sent* it.
> (Is. 55:11 ESVS)

Our conscience and natural loves act like handholds. Through them, God reveals his righteousness and steadfast love. Just as we can sear our conscience, we can break or bury our natural loves. Friendships collapse, family relationships go awry, and romantic love tragically falters and fails. Something inside us craves to be restored to loving righteousness. Who hasn't made the statement "That isn't fair!" Why do we consume movie after movie where broken relationships get fixed? God's handholds speak into our hearts and lead us back to him.

The Hebrew word for God's jealousy, *qannāʾ*, is used only six times and uniquely in reference only to him. His jealous love for us is nothing like human jealousy. He knows we need to love him in return or we will die. However cruelly life deals with us, his covenant love persists. It never fails.

> ¹ And God spoke all these words, saying,
> ² "I am the LORD your God, who brought you out of the land of Egypt, out of the house of slavery."
> ³ "You shall have no other gods before me."
> ⁴ "You shall not make for yourself a carved image, or any likeness of anything that is in heaven above, or that is in the earth beneath, or that is in the water under the earth. ⁵ You shall not bow down to them or serve them, for I the LORD your God am a *jealous* {*qannāʾ*} God, visiting the iniquity of the fathers on the children to the third and the fourth generation of those who *hate* {*śānēʾ*} me, ⁶ but showing *steadfast love* {*ḥesed̪*} to thousands of those who *love* {*ʾāhab̪*} me and keep my commandments." (Ex. 20:1-6 ESVS)

GK H7862 | S H7067 קַנָּא *qannāʾ* (kan-naw´) 6x a. [root of: 7868; cf. 7861]. jealous; an adjective or title used exclusively of God, focusing on his desire for exclusive relationships.[5]

GK H7863 | S H7068 קִנְאָה *qinʾāh* (kin-aw´) 43x n.f. [7861]. jealousy, envy, zeal.[6]

GK H8533 | S H8130 שָׂנֵא *śānēʾ* (saw-nay´) 148x v. [root of: 2190, 6171, 6176, 8534, 8535; 10686]. Q to hate, be an enemy; Qp to be unloved; N to be hated, be shunned; P to be an adversary, be a foe; "hate" can be active, as an enemy or adversary; or passive, as someone unloved or shunned. » abhor; despise;[7]

What about the people God "hates," like Esau in Genesis? God didn't hate Esau like we hate. The Hebrew for "hate" means enemy, adversary, or to shun and give no love. Before creating us, a timeless, ever-loving God knew who would and would not love him. We are his image and we will seek to love something even if it is not him! Why else do we pursue beauty or some other aspect of satisfying form? We will fill in our heart that void meant for only him, and it won't be his love.

Compare these three words translated as hate in Genesis, Malachi, and Romans. The English word hate fails to communicate the original context, meaning simply to detest. Do you notice the difference between Esau's hate for Jacob and God's hate for Esau? Particularly in this passage, Esau refers to his descendants, the Edomites, just as Jacob refers to the Israelite. Esau took wives and their religious practices and gods to fill God's void in him.

⁴¹ Now Esau *hated* {*śāṭam*} Jacob because of the blessing with which his father had blessed him, and Esau said to himself, "The days of mourning for my father are approaching; then I will kill my brother Jacob." (Gen. 27:41 ESVS)

² "I have *loved* {*ʾāhaḇ*} you," says the LORD. But you say, "How have you *loved* {*ʾāhaḇ*} us?" "Is not Esau Jacob's brother?" declares the LORD. "Yet I have *loved* {*ʾāhaḇ*} Jacob ³ but Esau I have *hated* {*śānēʾ*}. I have laid waste his hill country and left his heritage to jackals of the desert." (Mal. 1:2-3 ESVS)

¹³ As it is written, "Jacob I loved, but Esau I *hated* {*miseō*}." (Rom. 9:13 ESVS)

GK H8475 | S H7852 שָׂטַם *śāṭam* (saw-tam´) 6x v. [5378; cf. 8476]. Q to hold a grudge, hold hostility toward.⁸

GK G3631 | S G3404 μισέω *miseō* (mis-eh´-o) 40x to hate, regard with ill-will, Mt. 5:43, 44; 10:22; to detest, abhor, Jn. 3:20; Rom. 7:15; in NT to regard with less affection, love less, esteem less, Mt. 6:24; Lk. 14:26 » hate.⁹

Don't think for a moment that God abandoned his love for Esau. He embraces every prodigal who returns. Remember Ruth the Moabite redeemed by Boaz and Rahab the Canaanite prostitute in Jericho are ancestors of Jesus himself. They were not Israelites, but they were drawn by God's love. If Cain had given his heart to the Lord, would he not have accepted him? He hates our evil ways while steadfastly loving us. God is love, not hate. He has not rigged everlasting life against any of us.

Some actually believe God doesn't love everyone.[10] This erroneous conclusion results from profound torture of the Scripture and a violation of logic and reason.[11] How can God hate anyone if he tells us to love our neighbors as ourselves? Does he command us to do something he cannot? The plain-sense understanding of John 3:16 must necessarily stand. *God loves us all*. Salvation occurs the instant we love him in return, according to Philippians.

> 16 "For God so loved the world, that he gave his only Son, that whoever believes in him should not perish but have eternal life." (John 3:16 ESVS)

> 8 But let us, who are of the day, be sober, putting on the breastplate of faith and love; and for an helmet, the hope of salvation. 9 For God hath not appointed us to wrath, but to obtain salvation by our Lord Jesus Christ, 10 Who died for us, that, whether we wake or sleep, we should live together with him. (1Th. 5:8-10 KJVS)

Does Islam foster love? As far as I can determine, the Quran never says Allah *is* love. Muslims never know for sure that he loves them until they die with more accumulated good deeds than bad. Entrance into paradise and receiving Allah's love hinges on work alone, not unconditional love. Allah also tells Muslims to hate unbelievers. Scripture never teaches that God loves us *if* we do so and so. What we do can please or displease him, but like the father of the prodigal son, he *never* stops loving us.

Humans have a propensity to think life should become peachy when we know and experience God's love. I did. At around four, I stepped out of my pew, walked the aisle to the front of small packed church where my pastor led me in my first prayer to God. Stacy was also very young when she accepted him. I still vividly remember God's love washing all over me. Life seemed so wonderful until our newfound love for God crashed headlong into this world we broke.

Stacy and I met and married while I was in college, studying for medical school. With medical degree finally in hand, we moved on to pediatric residency at Oklahoma University in Tulsa. From there, I brought Stacy and our first little girl to El Dorado, Arkansas, where I set up a solo general pediatrics practice yet continued the Level III NICU medicine in which I was proficient.

Not long after moving, Laura was born with severe developmental disabilities. She would never speak, sit, crawl, or doing anything more than a three-month-old baby. The structural brain defects eventually led to a brain bleed and caused her death at twenty-four. Stacy and I cared for her ourselves at home all those years. Standing around her on a ventilator, we loved her one last time before we had to let her go.

Does a loving God *do* bad things? If he does love us, why did he allow her to die? Like many Christians, our silver spoon faith mistakenly led us to treat God like a genie in a bottle. We exercised our "faith" in prayer. Several times we took her on long trips to a now-discredited healing ministry. Each time we returned broken-hearted with Laura unhealed.

God's faith message has nothing to do with gritting your teeth and hanging on persistently until we "bother" him enough to give us what we want. The verse in Hebrews was etched on our heart. "Faith is the substance of things hoped for, the evidence of things not seen." It felt good to say, but hollow when Laura's little body remain unchanged. We were wounded.

Christians tend to pray for a perfect life here and now as though the whole reason God exists is to make us as comfortable as possible. Aren't we deserving of the terrible world we chose? Isn't he a genie that comes out of the lamp we have rubbed with our prayers? These false sentiments make the world think God is not good or powerful or both. We forget our context of a chosen separation from God.

We are supposed to pray, but gritting our faith teeth, asking or even commanding God to do what we want is not faith. That's why Jesus said faith need be no larger than a mustard seed. You just can't try harder when faith appears to fail.

Jesus lived and walked as a man. He was not a magician with mystical powers. Jesus's faith was perfect because he *loved* his Father no matter what he directed him to do or say. There was no magic or method in the sometimes apparently ridiculous ways he healed. The imagery we misunderstand actually tries to teach us what the substance of faith is.

> [20] He said to them, "Because of your little faith. For truly, I say to you, if you have faith like a grain of mustard seed, you will say to this mountain, 'Move from here to there,' and it will move, and nothing will be impossible for you." (Matt. 17:20 ESVS)
>
> [19] "It is like a grain of mustard seed that a man took and sowed in his garden, and it grew and became a tree, and the birds of the air made nests in its branches." (Luke 13:19 ESVS)
>
> [6] And the Lord said, "If you had faith like a grain of mustard seed, you could say to this mulberry tree, 'Be uprooted and planted in the sea,' and it would obey you." (Luke 17:6 ESVS)

What does moving a mountain, growing a mustard seed tree large enough to host many birds, or casting a mulberry tree to the sea have to do with measuring faith? We need look no further than the story of Shadrach, Meshach, and Abednego in Nebuchadnezzar's fiery furnace. They knew God loved them and that *was* the substance of their faith. Whether perishing in the flames or losing our sick child, faith tells us God's love is sure. Circumstances like Laura's terrible situation cannot be the measure we use to know he loves us.

16 Shadrach, Meshach, and Abednego answered and said to the king, "O Nebuchadnezzar, we have no need to answer you in this matter. 17 If this be so, our God whom we serve is able to deliver us from the burning fiery furnace, and he will deliver us out of your hand, O king. 18 But if not, be it known to you, O king, that we will not serve your gods or worship the golden image that you have set up." (Dan. 3:16-18 ESVS)

God's love is decisive love, the substance of our faith, and the only cure for our broken being.

CHAPTER EIGHT

Forgiveness

Most of the Circle of Love comes from 1 Corinthians 13. The peripheral aspects derive from God's central character of timeless agape love. It endures because he never sleeps or slumbers. Peter misunderstood agape love at first. Three times when Jesus asked "Do you love me?" he responded with friendship love. Peter did come to understand later what Jesus meant.

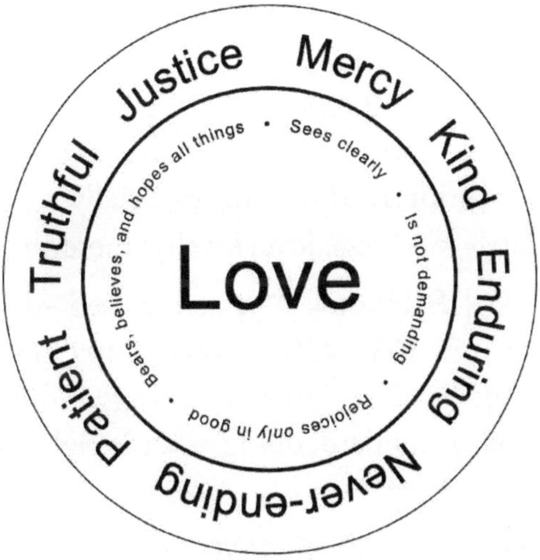
Justice
Mercy
Kind
Enduring
Never-ending
Patient
Truthful
Sees clearly
Is not demanding
Rejoices only in good
Bears, believes, and hopes all things
Love

Forgiveness

Justice and mercy come from Psalm 85:10. The ESV, NKJV, and Amplified Bible translations reveal the rich relationship between justice and mercy. The Hebrew words for righteousness mean justice while peace means a place of safety.

> [10] *Steadfast love* {*ḥeseḏ*} and *faithfulness* {*ʾemeṯ*} meet;
> *righteousness* {*ṣeḏeq*} and *peace* {*šālom*}
> *kiss* {*nāšaq*} each other.
> (Psa. 85:10 ESVS)

> [10] *Mercy* {*ḥeseḏ*} and *truth* {*ʾemeṯ*} have met together;
> *Righteousness* {*ṣeḏeq*} and *peace* {*šālom*}
> have *kissed* {*nāšaq*}.
> (Psa. 85:10 NKJV)

> [10] *Mercy and loving-kindness* {*ḥeseḏ*} and *truth* {*ʾemeṯ*}
> have met together; *righteousness* {*ṣeḏeq*} and
> *peace* {*šālom*} have *kissed* {*nāšaq*} each other.
> (Psa. 85:10 AMP)

GK H2876 | S H2617 חֶסֶד *ḥeseḏ* (kheh´-sed) 249x n.m. [root of: 1213, 2877, 2878?, 2883; cf. 2874]. unfailing love, loyal love, devotion, kindness, often based on a prior relationship, especially a covenant relationship. » kindness; love; loyalty; mercy.[1]

GK H7406 | S H6664 צֶדֶק *ṣeḏeq* (seh´-dek) 123x n.m. [root of: 155, 4900, 7408, 7409; cf. 7405]. righteousness, justice, rightness, acting according to a proper (God's) standard, doing what is right, being in the right. » justice;[2]

GK H8934 | S H7965 שָׁלוֹם *šālom* (shaw-lome´) 237x n.m. [root of: 58, 94, 8976, 8979, 8984, 8985; cf.

8966; 10720]. peace, safety, prosperity, well-being; intactness, wholeness; peace can have a focus of security, safety which can bring feelings of satisfaction, well-being, and contentment. » completeness; health; peace;[3]

GK H5975 | S H5401 נָשַׁק *nāšaq* (naw-shak´) 30x v. [root of: 5965]. Q to kiss; P to kiss (repeatedly or intensely); a kiss can show familial or romantic affection, as well as homage and submission.

GK H622 | S H571 אֱמֶת *ʾemet̞* (eh´-meth) 127x n.f. [root of: 624; cf. 586]. faithfulness, reliability, trustworthiness; truth, what conforms to reality in contrast to what is false; "the book of truth" is a reliable book, referring to heavenly scroll detailing future things. » faithfulness; truth.[4]

Within his timeless context, God can never be anything other than what he is. His name is "I AM," which means he never changes. He is perfect in every way because his love is always unconditional. All creation lies within his sovereign boundary of authority, but saying "Sovereign Lord" is simply redundant. Saying "Loving God" describes everything about him and who he is. There is none like him because there never was a love like his.

Adam and Eve's disobedience in the garden parted all of us from God, but it never changed his love. Their failure did not take God by surprise. Before he called everything into existence, he knew all that would happen. Rescue implies action after the catastrophe, while redemption was his plan to completely recover and restore us before he started the clock of time ticking. Romans describes the problem and the solution.

> [19] For as by the one man's disobedience the many were made sinners, so by the one man's obedience the many will be made righteous. (Rom. 5:19 ESVS)

The first "Adam" failed. Jesus is called the "second Adam." Though born a man through Mary, he was not a son of Adam. Mary became pregnant through the Holy Spirit, which means Jesus is the Son of God. His exclusive title, "Son of Man" means he is the God-man. Because God is his father, he is *not* a sinner like us. But his human body could die since he was born just like we were. Adam could not save us, but Jesus humanly dying in our place could. Unlike Adam, Father God declared he would not allow Jesus to remain in the grave. His human resurrection means we too can be "born again."

> [7] Truly no man can ransom another,
>   or give to God the price of his life,
> [8] for the ransom of their life is costly
>   and can never suffice,
> [9] that he should live on forever
>   and never see the pit.
> (Psa. 49:7-9 ESVS)
>
> [25] For David says concerning him,[5]
>   "'I saw the Lord always before me,
>   for he is at my right hand that I may not
>   be shaken;
> [26] therefore my heart was glad, and my tongue

> rejoiced;
>   my flesh also will dwell in hope.
> 27 For you will not abandon my soul to Hades,
>   or let your Holy One see corruption...'"
> (Acts 2:25-27 ESVS)

> 34 And as for the fact that he raised him from the dead, no more to return to corruption, he has spoken in this way,
>   "'I will give you the holy and sure blessings of
>   David.'"
> 35 Therefore he says also in another psalm,
>   "'You will not let your Holy One see corruption'..."
> (Acts 13:34-35 ESVS)

Jesus's flesh could take our curse and corruption to Sheol, but because his spirit and soul remained holy, God would not leave him in the grave. When he raised Jesus, his body was made incorruptible. Never again could he die for us, and never will there be another like him who could. Anyone who unequivocally abandons Jesus after *sincerely* accepting him as savior has no alternative but to stand before God and receive the justice due him.

Charles Templeton was Billy Graham's dear friend and co-evangelist in the 1940s Youth for Christ evangelistic explosion. Some said he was destined to be greatest evangelist ever. Imagine the shock in 1957 when Templeton declared himself an agnostic. By 1966, he turned fully to atheism in *Farewell to God: My Reasons for Rejecting the Christian Faith*. Lee Strobel's movie A

Case for Faith recounts his whole story. Templeton died in 2001 without Christ as far as we know.

In 1984, after preaching for nineteen years, Daniel Edwin Barker abandoned his faith. He and his wife, both now committed atheists, served as co-presidents of the Freedom From Religion Foundation. Not satisfied in their own non-belief, they and their organization actively oppose Christianity and promote atheism. If Dan Barker dies without Christ, he certainly has no hope.

Some doubt that a person can "lose their faith." They might question whether Templeton or Barker were ever saved in the first place. Perhaps Templeton repented at the very last? We see men only through their words and deeds. Their heart remains visible only for God to know when the prodigal becomes apostate. Yet, the mere presence of these verses in Hebrews suggests we *can* walk away from the Lord.

> 4 For it is impossible, in the case of those who have once been enlightened, who have tasted the heavenly gift, and have shared in the Holy Spirit, 5 and have tasted the goodness of the word of God and the powers of the age to come, 6 and then have fallen away, to restore them again to repentance, since they are crucifying once again the Son of God to their own harm and holding him up to contempt. (Heb. 6:4-6 ESVS)

Conversely, this verse also means God loves us so much he will *let* us walk away! Forcing his love upon us would change his fundamental nature, and God never changes. The oxymoron "conditional love" is an absolute contradiction in terms that cannot apply to him.

Jesus stands like an open door between justice and mercy, inviting us to come inside the circle where the Father, the Son, the Holy Spirit, and all who believe each give and accept love. Accepting God's invitation to join this perichoretic love feast is part one. Part two necessarily requires we love not only those already inside, but everyone in the same way. We must forgive like he forgives. That's harder because such forgiveness requires our conscious choice.

Our youngest daughter Laura died on April 24, 2012 at twenty-four from a massive brain hemorrhage. We hired a nurse to help us years earlier upon a friend's referral. She and Stacy even became good friends. About four months before Laura passed, Stacy walked in on her cursing our wheelchair-bound Laura and striking repeatedly in the face. It all ended with the police leading her away in handcuffs.

Developmentally, she was no more than three months, but at twenty-four, the court considered Laura a disabled adult. Her caretaker could not be charged with child abuse. After serving six months' incarceration and year or so on probation, she was free. During all this, we found she hid a prior conviction before we hired her. Did the force of her repeated blows, contribute to or cause her brainstem bleed? We will probably never know.

Forgiving her didn't produce any warm fuzzies. We struggled, but knew we had to forgive even if she didn't ask. God both forgives and forgets[6] when we repent. We cannot forget, but still must forgive. That nurse may well be a sister in Christ walking with us in heaven someday. No doubt there will be many other similarly profound and tearful reconciliations in heaven.

We long for the day when God changes us forever. Imagine no forgiveness need ever be sought because none will ever be required. Along with a new name, a new body, a perfect heart, we will have a mind unable to even think evil thoughts. Sin dies all because of God's decisive love. His right to create us in the first place comes from his love and his loving power to redeem and remake us.

> [50] I tell you this, brothers: flesh and blood cannot inherit the kingdom of God, nor does the perishable inherit the imperishable. [51] Behold! I tell you a mystery. We shall not all sleep, but we shall all be changed, [52] in a moment, in the twinkling of an eye, at the last trumpet. For the trumpet will sound, and the dead will be raised imperishable, and we shall be changed. [53] For this perishable body must put on the imperishable, and this mortal body must put on immortality. [54] When the perishable puts on the imperishable, and the mortal puts on immortality, then shall come to pass the saying that is written:
>
> "Death is swallowed up in victory."
> [55] "O death, where is your victory?
>   O death, where is your sting?"
> [56] The sting of death is sin, and the power of sin is the law. [57] But thanks be to God, who gives us the victory

through our Lord Jesus Christ. (1Cor. 15:50-57 ESVS)

CHAPTER NINE

Prayer

C. S. Lewis accurately described the problem of pain in Mere Christianity. Pain afflicts everyone. Nonbelievers, as well as all who believe in, trust in, and rely upon God, can be trapped into this line of thinking.

> "If God were good, He would wish to make His creatures perfectly happy, and if God were almighty, He would be able to do what He wished. But the creatures are not happy. Therefore, God lacks either goodness, or power, or both." This is the problem of pain, in its simplest form.[1]

How we think about the problem of pain relegates everyone into two groups. Those who experience life's ills from one event to the next often think they deserve better. When an all-powerful God doesn't make everything right, he becomes the *cause* of pain. They live with high expectations that medicine, politics, government, or something stops our hurting. They are the first to yell, "That's not fair!" This group invisibly harbors the impression that mankind is not responsible for its awful situation. Somehow God is at fault.

I would expect nonbelievers to naturally think this way, but Christians can and do get snared also. Just think about how we pray. When painful things threaten, do they approach God as a genie rather than a loving Father? Do they rub the lamp with pious words, hoping God will pop out and grant them their every wish to avoid or relieve pain? Unfortunately, life's chain of painful events requires many repeated trips to the lamp and more than three wishes.

The lamp bearer sees God only through the lens of "answered prayer." God is not a loving Father, but simply one who sends their packaged fixes. Clearly, the "name it, claim it" prosperity gospel bears much responsibility for reducing God to a delivery man. My prayers to fix mine and Stacy's pain over little Laura caused me to reduce him to that.

If life is simply a string of packaged fixes, what will a relationship with God look like in heaven? Is it then we somehow start seeing him as a loving Father?

We struggled for years when Laura faced one challenge after another. All of us experience pain, which came because we separated ourselves from God. Packaged prayer parcels never would have fixed the prodigal son. Our Father stands ready to embrace us with continuous, decisive love.

Do we approach God like this woman approached the judge when we pray?

> ¹ And he told them a parable to the effect that they ought always to pray and not lose heart. ² He said, "In a certain city there was a judge who neither feared God nor respected man. ³ And there was a widow in that city who kept coming to him and saying, 'Give me justice against my adversary.' ⁴ For a while he refused, but afterward he said to himself, 'Though I neither fear God nor respect man, ⁵ yet because this widow keeps bothering me, I will give her justice, so that she will not beat me down by her continual coming.'" ⁶ And the Lord said, "Hear what the unrighteous judge says. ⁷ And will not God give justice to his elect, who cry to him day and night? Will he delay long over them? ⁸ I tell you, he will give justice to them speedily. Nevertheless, when the Son of Man comes, will he find faith on earth?" (Luke 18:1-8 ESVS)

Jesus is *not* telling us to hound the Father the way the widow pursued the unjust judge! This verse instructs us to believe that God hears our prayers because he is just. Jesus never taught us to bug God until he gives what we want.

The relationship between the Father, the Son, and the Holy Spirit is perichoretic. The term perichoresis comes from the Greek word perichoresi, meaning "rotation." It is a composite of two other Greek words "peri," meaning around and "chorien," meaning to give away. The Father, the Son, and the Holy Spirit each give love to and receive love from the other two.

> ⁴¹ And he withdrew from them about a stone's throw, and knelt down and prayed, ⁴² saying, "Father, if you are willing, remove this cup from me. Nevertheless, not my will, but yours, be done." (Luke 22:41-42 ESVS)

Often we misinterpret Jesus's prayer in the garden as a sign of his reluctance and fear of the pain of the cross. The better understanding of this points to his pending separation from the Father and Holy Spirit when he took our punishment to the grave. Clearly, Jesus's perichoretic relationship with the Father and Holy Spirit caused him to be with them, often away from everyone else. He knew his part in our redemption before creation, so how could he doubt his own plan?

Hebrews says that faith is the substance of things hoped for and the evidence of things not seen. Out of desperation, I hoped for Laura's healing, mistakenly thinking that was faith. I rubbed that lamp many, many times because my faith was in his power and not in his love. If God had answered like I wanted, would I ever become part of his perichoresis?

I could not find the term perichoresis at dictionary.com or recent printed dictionaries I own. In my 1941 copy of Webster's Second Edition of the New International Dictionary of the English Language,[2] perichoresis equates to circumcision of the heart.

> ¹⁶ Circumcise therefore the foreskin of your heart, and be no longer stubborn. (Deut. 10:16 ESVS)

⁶ And the LORD your God will circumcise your heart and the heart of your offspring, so that you will love the LORD your God with all your heart and with all your soul, that you may live. (Deut. 30:6 ESVS)

⁴ Circumcise yourselves to the LORD;
    remove the foreskin of your hearts,
        O men of Judah and inhabitants of Jerusalem;
    lest my wrath go forth like fire,
        and burn with none to quench it,
            because of the evil of your deeds."
(Jer. 4:4 ESVS)

Circumcision is all about being part of the perichoretic dance within his circle of love. When I pray now, I first tell my heart to listen for him. Next, I tell the Father my heart is his! Finally, I tell myself to share his decisive love with others.

CHAPTER TEN

Final Thoughts

1 Timothy 4:4 says that everything created by God is good. The original word translated "good" bears a richness that escapes our English. In various other verses, it means "beautiful, good, of good quality or disposition, fertile, rich, useful, profitable, it is well, excellent, choice, select, goodly, it is pleasant, delightful, just, full measure; honorable, distinguished, possessing moral excellence, worthy, upright, virtuous, what is good and right, a good deed, rectitude, virtue, right, duty, propriety, benefit, favor."

No God, but a good God could create only good things. He is blameless for the world's ills, and we are stupid to think our pitiful circumstances resulted from anything but our own evil. Those blaming God, curse and raise a fist at him for the very freedom he gave them to walk away.

Holiness means different things to different peoples and religions. Many paintings of Jesus, the apostles, and revered saints depict holiness by posture, facial expression, direction of gaze,

Final Thoughts

and, most importantly, a halo. That kind of holiness is hollow, and of no help to anyone.

A good God is holy because he is wholly good. His goodness comes from his steadfast love for us. He never fails to love. He doesn't walk away disgusted like me when I got angry with my daughter. God lovingly corrects but never leaves. We are all bruised reeds, which he promises never to break. He is our example of what we should be.

If you aren't broken yet, I can assure you this world will eventually give you your turn. You *will* need a loving Father someday. He patiently waits because he's in for the long game. It may take decades, but he will work you into a place where you face your need for his love. You may never respond, even with his best efforts. He loves you regardless, and he *won't* manipulate you into heaven.

Now may be your time. If his decisive love beckons, you should respond. Everyone gets the same relationship with the Father no matter how long they've known him or how bad they've been. You need only ask him into your heart where he'll start changing you immediately.

Just ask him. *Just ask*. He'll make you all good again.

Appendix & Supplementals

Laura's Story 65

Bookmark Timeline Reference 71

Our Spiritual Anatomy 79

Guide To Kohlenberger/Mounce Hebrew-Aramaic Dictionary ... 91

Acknowledgments .... -7

Bibliography & Endnotes 95

Laura's Story

We lived out Lewis's statement through our Laura, who died in 2012. The quote below from Lewis that I shared in Chapter 1 {of *Between Justice & Mercy with Related Essays}*, is painfully close for Stacy and me. Laura set my life on a different course. I doubt this book would ever have been written, if not for her.

> "If God were good, He would wish to make His creatures perfectly happy, and if God were almighty, He would be able to do what He wished. But the creatures are not happy. Therefore, God lacks either goodness, or power, or both." This is the problem of pain, in its simplest form.[1]

Every part of our life will help you understand how this book really started. When Laura died, my heart was left with all the why's. The answers started coming as I pressed into his love. I'm not seminary trained, but I take great comfort in knowing that C. S. Lewis was not either. God is very capable, but he cannot snap his fingers and instantly change things. His love puts boundaries on what he will or will not and can or cannot do.

Pain is not something God caused. We own that. In its awfulness, pain opens a crack in us where his light and love can shine. He wastes nothing to press in close, and we cannot stop him loving us no matter how we injure him. The only way pain ends is if God accepted our justice—the justice that *we* rightly earned.

He is good. He does want to make us happy. His plan is playing out to bring us back to him, and most people will not come easily. In the end he will redeem all who ask and then end their pain forever.

> [8] ¶ Woe unto them that join house to house, that lay field to field, till there be no place, that they may be placed alone in the midst of the earth!
> (Is. 25:8 KJV)

Laura. I just retired from general pediatrics after thirty-six years. I graduated medical school in 1983, and I started my career after residency in Oklahoma.

Stacy and I married young. She was twenty, and I was just nineteen. I started medical school at just twenty-one. Though my family was poor when I was young, my dad built his natural gas pipeline business into a three-state operation. He dropped out of school in the eighth grade, and he and mom dreamed of giving their sons the opportunities they never had.

Stacy's father, Gilbert Morris, taught English at Ouachita Baptist University in Arkadelphia where we lived. A popular and prolific historical fiction novelist, he authored well over two hundred books. He preached part-time filling in mostly where needed at small Baptist churches.

I accepted the Lord as my personal savior at the age of four. Stacy, too, came to know him when she was very young. We follow him still as we enter our sixties.

Andrea was born in 1984, while we were still in residency in Oklahoma. I brought my family back to a small Arkansas town near the Louisiana border. Laura was born there after our first year in solo practice. During Stacy's pregnancy with Laura, things took an unexpected turn.

Our little Laura was born with fetal isotretinoin embryopathy because Stacy was on a prescription medicine called Accutane. Stacy got pregnant even though we were taking double precautions. Those nine months were awful. We prayed.

She never progressed developmentally beyond three months. Stacy and I cared for her ourselves at home until she passed away at age twenty-four.

By age thirteen, Laura's choking during feeding became so bad that she could only feed through a GI button in her stomach. Serious implications following the surgery to place that feeding port in her abdomen resulted in a one-month PICU stay. Four more surgeries followed before she was discharged. Stacy and I stayed by her side. I slept on the floor by her bed, Stacy took the one convertible chair, and our family helped us by taking shifts with her.

She recovered, but from then on, the years didn't seem kind. She developed seizures. On a number of occasions, Stacy and I worked sometimes for several hours to stop them. It took large doses of anticonvulsant to get them stopped, and they occurred more frequently toward the end.

As if it weren't difficult enough being a father to a disabled child, I was also her physician. There were only about three hundred other children with her condition. Though my residence training was good, nothing could have prepared me for what we faced.

Finally, on April 24, 2012, Laura passed away with all her family all around her. A sudden brain bleed led to emergency surgery on a Friday. Though Saturday looked better, she crashed on Sunday, and by Monday we knew she was gone. On Tuesday, we handed our little Laura back to our Lord.

I have already made the case for timelessness and how it is not the same as eternity. My understanding of the difference came as Stacy and I were standing in the funeral home making final arrangements with the secretary there. As we handed over a poem—really a prayer—which was penned in my pain for Laura, God proved to us he had heard our cries.

Laura passed away on April 24, 2012. The poem was dated April 24, 1992. I remembered back when I had written it how the Lord urged me forward. I cried out to him with the same intensity as my pain. God knew the day Laura would come to him. He had nudged me to write the poem exactly twenty years before then.

In that instant, God affirmed to Stacy and me he had been with us all that time. How else could those two dates be exactly twenty years apart? Seasoned Christian believers that we were, and having done medical missions worldwide, we were suddenly and keenly aware of how much God loved us.

I know God is timeless. I know we are eternal. I know he loves us and he had no part in Laura's illness. We live in a broken world of man's own making. Believing that anyone else caused our own pain is no small lie. God never intended our world to be what it is.

Christians seeking to make their life smooth, painless, and well-provisioned should stop. Though he is coming and will see to those things, remember that *he himself is the prize*. There is no substitute.

Forever And A Day For Laura Michelle
by Ron Smith, MD, April 24, 1992

…now being confident of this, that he who began a good work in you will carry it on to completion until the day of Christ Jesus.—Philippians 1:6

I started praying for a little child the other day.
   'Cause I was sure that was God's way
To heal that little one and make her whole.
   I was sure of this royal goal.
Her little body was twisted and turned.
   Oh, how in my heart the desire burned,
For her wholeness all at once to see,
   And then to be all that she could be.

As I prayed, the Holy One spoke quietly
   To my inner man on bended knee.
How long will you wait, how long will you believe
   For this miracle that in your heart I've conceived?
I thought only momentarily, and said,
   God, I'm your servant, I wait in your stead
If it be a day, a month, a year or three,
   I'll wait, I'll wait, I'll wait, this miracle to see!
Days, months, years passed by,
   And it seemed the Lord waited, I don't know why,
To heal my little girl, such a precious sight,
   So small and frail, sometimes I would just cry.
But His words to me would echo,
   And in my spirit man, I knew it would be so.
How long will I wait, how long will I believe,
   For this miracle that in my heart you've conceived?
Forever And A Day,
   That's the only way
stand in faith, for this my child.
   Though it seems her healing hides,
      it will only be a little while.

Bookmark Timeline Reference

This came from my book *Between Justice & Mercy with Related Essays*. Jesus prophesied not only his death and resurrection, but that he would be in the grave for three days. His prophecy is the most important in Scripture. If it is not precisely true, then he is not the Son of God. The timeline is a composite of three chapters and there is so much more you need to know than what I could cram into the timeline bookmark. Below is the image of the Last Passover Bookmark and the reference key.

The Last Passover Nisan 3790

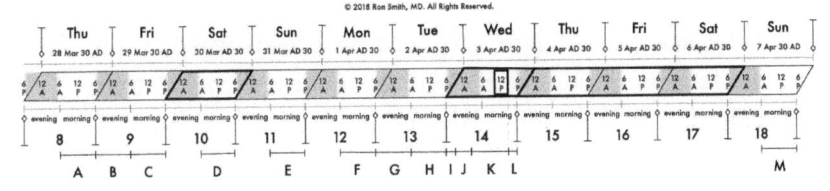

© 2018 Ron Smith, MD. All Rights Reserved.

Thu	Fri	Sat	Sun	Mon	Tue	Wed	Thu	Fri	Sat	Sun
28 Mar 30 AD	29 Mar 30 AD	30 Mar 30 AD	31 Mar 30 AD	1 Apr AD 30	2 Apr AD 30	3 Apr AD 30	4 Apr AD 30	5 Apr AD 30	6 Apr AD 30	7 Apr AD 30

8 — A | 9 — B, C | 10 — D | 11 — E | 12 — F, G | 13 — H, I, J | 14 — K, L | 15 | 16 | 17 | 18 — M

8 Nisan (morning), 9 Nisan (evening). Jesus Travels to Bethany to stay with Mary, Martha, and Lazarus, where he and the disciples eat with them. Jerusalem is less than two miles walk.

> **A. John 12:1** Six days before the Passover, Jesus comes to Bethany.
>
> **B. John 12:2-8** They gave a dinner for him there. Martha served. Mary anointed Jesus's feet, then wiped them with her hair. Judas objects. Jesus says she is anointing him for his burial.

9 Nisan (morning), 10 Nisan (dusk). News of Jesus's arrival spreads and crowds come out to see both Jesus and Lazarus. The weekly Sabbath begins at dusk that Friday.

> **C. John 12:9-11** A large crowd showed up in Bethany to see Lazarus who had been raised from the dead. The chief priests wanted to kill him and Jesus also. But many were believing.

10 Nisan (morning), 10 Nisan (before dusk). Jesus rides into Jerusalem on Sabbath day as cheer him on with palm branches. Bethany is less than two miles away so traveling there does not break Jewish law. Less conspicuous is the brief visit to the empty Temple. This is nothing less than the Jesus proclaiming that the "lamb is in the House of God" fulfilling Exodus 12:3.

> **D.1 John 12:12-15** A large crowd heard Jesus was coming to Jerusalem. So they took branches of palm trees calling out "Hosanna! Blessed is he who comes in the name of the Lord, even the King of Israel!"
> **D.3 John 12:23** Jesus tells them its time for the Son of Man to be glorified.
> **D.4 John 12:28** Jesus prays "Father, glorify your name," and a voice from heaven cries "I have glorified it, and I will glorify it again."

> **D.5 Mark 11:11** Jesus enters the temple but it is empty. He looks around seeing no one, then leaves with the disciples.

11 Nisan (morning). Jesus finds no fruit on the fig tree. The tree will never again produce fruit. He drives out those using the Temple to sell ahead of Passover. Israel is the fig tree.

> **E. Mark 11:12-16** The following day, as they came from Bethany, he was hungry. Along the way there was a fig tree with no fruit as it was not the season for figs. He says, "May no one ever eat fruit from you again." They continued on to the temple where Jesus began to drive out both buyers and sellers. He would not allow anyone to even carry anything through the temple."

12 Nisan (morning). The angry Pharisees, without income from the merchants selling in the Temple, confront Jesus. He finds no fruit on the fig tree (Israel). The tree will never again produce fruit. He drives out those using the Temple to sell. The fig tree now withered represents their sad, spiritual state. Jesus tells of Israel and Jerusalem's fate. The Chief Priests are actively plotting to kill Jesus.

> **F1. Mark 11:20-21** The next morning passing the fig tree again on their way to the temple, they saw it withered away at its roots.
> **F2. Mark 11:27-29** The chief priest corner him and ask "By what authority are you doing these things, or who gave you this authority to do them?" Jesus said, "I will ask you one question; answer me, and I will tell you by what authority I do these things. Was the baptism of John from heaven or from man? Answer me."

F3. Mark 13:1-2 Upon leaving the temple someone remarks about the wonderful stones and buildings. Jesus replies, "Do you see these great buildings? There will not be left here one stone upon another that will not be thrown down."

F4. Mark 13:28-29 Jesus explains about the fig tree (Israel) that withered will live once again. When it does, we will know that the end is near, eat at the gates.

F5. Mark 14:1-2 It is two days before the Feast of Unleavened Bread. The chief priests and scribes were planning to arrest Jesus privately and kill him except they feared the people; "Not during the feast, lest there be an uproar from the people."

13 Nisan (evening). In one more day, Jesus's time comes. At Simon's house, a woman anoints him with nard, the same precious, aromatic oil used to anoint Aaron, the Ark of the Covenant, the Tent of Meeting, and all High Priests.

G1. Mark 14:3 While he was at Bethany in the house of Simon the leper, another woman came with a costly alabaster flask of ointment of pure nard and poured it over his head.

G2. Mark 14:10 Judas Iscariot goes to the chief priests to betray Jesus. They promised to give him money., and he waited for an opportunity.

13 Nisan (morning). The first day of Unleavened Bread refers to the Day of Preparation, not the first feast day. Because leaven was excluded from homes on the Day of Preparation also, many Jewish communities celebrate it as the first of eight days of Feast of Unleavened Bread, instead of seven.

H. Mark 14:12-16 The first day of Unleavened Bread, when they sacrificed the Passover lamb (this is the Day of Preparation of passover starting at dusk. At dusk just before dusk at the end of this day, the Passover lambs are sacrifices, then roast it as Passover began). And the disciples went to the city and found the upper room just as he said, and they prepared for the Passover which would be the next day.

14 Nisan (evening). Because this is the Day of Preparation of Passover, roast lamb is not present. Rather, the Lamb of God gives a new commandment of bread and wine. The bread is the bride price while the wine is purity of the bloodied *chuppah* cloth. This Last Supper is analogous to the *erusin* initiated by the Father of the Bridegroom after which we are forever his.

>**I1. Mark 14:17-18** In the evening on the Day of Preparation of Passover (what we call the Last Supper), Jesus said, "Truly, I say to you, one of you will betray me, one who is eating with me."
>
>**I2. Mark 14:22-24** Jesus breaks the bread which represents the bride price of his body which the disciples eat. Then he gives the wine representing the blood on the chuppah cloth that declares we are pure.
>
>**J1. Mark 14:26** They sang and then went to the Mount of Olives.
>
>**J2. Mark 14:32-33** There at Gethsemane he tells the disciples, "Sit here while I pray." He took Peter, James ,and John further on with him. He became greatly distressed and troubled.
>
>**J3. Mark 14:43** Judas comes with a crowd carrying swords and clubs from the chief priests, scribes, and elders.

J4. Mark 14:55 The whole council was seeking testimony against Jesus so they could put him to deathNo one testified. He remained silent when they asked, "Are you the Christ, the Son of the Blessed?" He says "I am, and you will see the Son of Man seated at the right hand of Power, and coming with the clouds of heaven."The high priest tore his garments and said,

J5. Mark 14:61–64 "What further witnesses do we need? You have heard his blasphemy. What is your decision?" The whole council condemned him to death. They had no capital authority to carry out the death sentence, however.

J6. Mark 14:72 The rooster crowed a second time. And Peter remembered Jesus words, "Before the rooster crows twice, you will deny me three times." He broke down crying.

14 Nisan (morning). Jesus is condemned, flogged, beaten, and finally nailed to the cross by the third Jewish hour (9 a.m.). By the sixth hour (3 p.m.), Jesus is dead having finished his work.

K1. Mark 15:1–2 Jesus was tried during the night but they led him away and delivered him over to Pilate who was the only one who could carry out the death sentence. Pilate asked, "Are you the King of the Jews?" Jesus answered, "You have said so."

K2. John 19:14 It was still the Day of Preparation of the Passover at the sixth hour (six o'clock). Pilate said to the Jews, "Behold your King!"

K3. John 19:16–18 So Pilate delivered him over to them to be crucified. Jesus carried his own cross to The Place of a Skull, known in Aramaic as Golgotha. There they crucified him and two others on either side of him.

K4. John 19:23–27 When the soldiers crucified Jesus, they divided his clothes four parts, one part for each soldier except for his tunic. Because it was just one piece the said, "Let us not tear it, but cast lots for it to see whose it shall be." This fulfilled the scripture that says, "They divided my garments among them, and for my clothing they cast lots." As they did this Jesus's mother and his mother's sister, Mary the wife of Clopas, and Mary Magdalene were watching. Jesus saw his mother and the disciple whom he loved standing nearby. He said to his mother, "Woman, behold, your son!" Then he said to the disciple, "Behold, your mother!" He took Mary into his own home.

14 Nisan (late afternoon) and 15 Nisan (dusk). Jesus is Jesus is removed from the cross, his body treated with spices and wrapped in linen, and he has been placed in a new grave.

L1. John 19:28–30 After Jesus knows all was now finished, he fulfills Scripture and says, "I thirst." They gave him sour wine on a sponge with a hyssop branch. When Jesus had received it, he said, "It is finished," and he bowed his head and died.

L2. Mark 15:37–39 Jesus uttered a loud cry, breathed his last and died. The temple curtain was torn in two, from top to bottom. The centurion facing him, saw this and said, "Truly this man was the Son of God!"

L3. Mark 15:43–45 Joseph of Arimathea was a respected council member, but who was also looking for the kingdom of God, asked Pilate for Jesus's body. Surprised Jesus had already died, he granted Jesus's body to Joseph after he confirmed it.

L4. John 19:31–34 Because it was the Day of Preparation of Passover, no bodies could remain on the cross on the Passover at dusk. Passover is a High Sabbath. That is why the Jews asked Pilate to break their legs so they would die quickly before dusk. So the soldiers broke the legs of the two beside Jesus who was already dead. They confirmed his death when blood and water poured out after piercing his side with a spear.

L5. Mark 15:46 Having bought a linen shroud, Joseph took him down, wrapped him in it and laid him in a tomb cut out of the rock. Then they rolled a stone against the tomb entrance.

18 Nisan (evening). As the weekly Sabbath wanes at dusk, Jesus rises from the dead as night falls. Most everyone is inside getting ready for bed. It is only at the first light of morning that several women find his grave empty.

M. Mark 16:2–7 Very early on Sunday, the first day of the week, they went to the tomb just as the sun had risen. While saying among themselves, "Who will roll away the stone for us from the entrance of the tomb?" they were started to see the large stone had been rolled back. At the tomb entrance on the right, they were alarmed when they saw a young man in a white robe. He told them, "Do not be alarmed. You seek Jesus of Nazareth, who was crucified. He has risen; he is not here. See the place where they laid him." He told them to go tell his disciples and Peter he has gone on before them to Galilee and that he would see them there as he had said.

Our Spiritual Anatomy

While it exists for us, mercy is not extended to angels. Our spiritual anatomy reveals much about how we are different from angels who have no body. Though we are very weak compared to those spiritual brothers, he created us alone in his image.

Body. When we smell and taste delicious food, our salivary glands produce the necessary secretions to chew and begin digestion. When we hear or see something frightening, it revs up our fight-or-flight response. Sensations are the connection of our body to the physical world around us.

The animal nature of our flesh has basic needs for food, space, sexual intercourse, etc. This animal nature drives us to meet all of its needs and wants. To see the flesh in action, one only needs to watch the daily activities of a mother with a baby. Most all the needs that she meets are those of the baby's flesh.

Our flesh is the visible and physical connection that we have with time and space. It is our common link to all the other animals in the world.

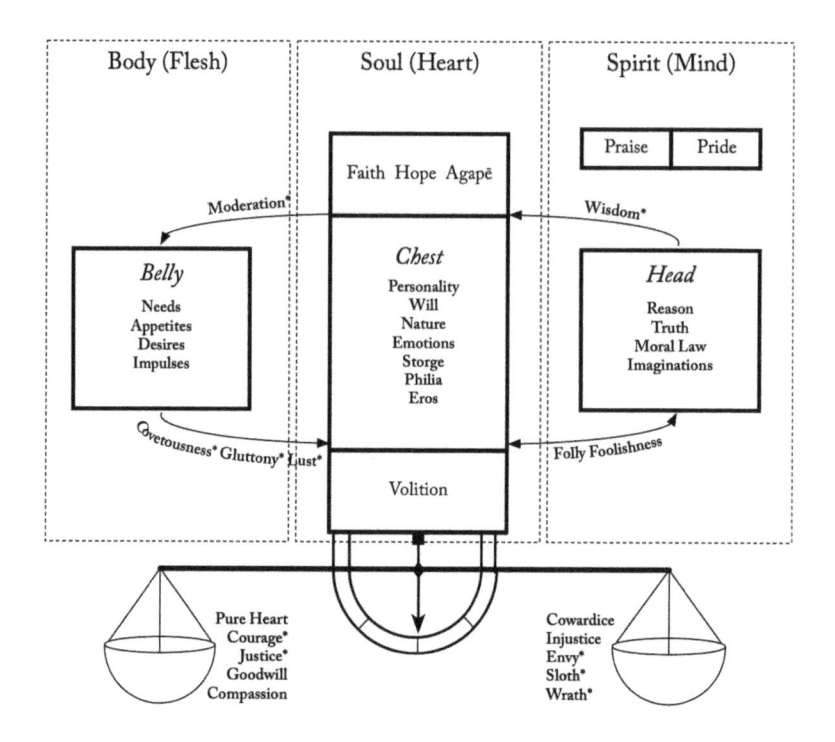

```
        Body (Flesh)          Soul (Heart)           Spirit (Mind)

                                                    ┌───────┬───────┐
                                                    │ Praise│ Pride │
                                                    └───────┴───────┘
                              Faith Hope Agapē
                    Moderation*                Wisdom*

         ┌──────────┐         Chest              ┌──────────┐
         │  Belly   │     Personality            │   Head   │
         │          │        Will                │          │
         │  Needs   │       Nature               │  Reason  │
         │ Appetites│      Emotions              │   Truth  │
         │ Desires  │       Storge               │Moral Law │
         │ Impulses │       Philia               │Imaginations│
         │          │         Eros               │          │
         └──────────┘                            └──────────┘
              Covetousness* Gluttony* Lust*         Folly Foolishness

                              Volition


           Pure Heart                              Cowardice
            Courage*                               Injustice
            Justice*                                 Envy*
            Goodwill                                 Sloth*
           Compassion                                Wrath*
```

Soul. In the soul, also known as our heart, lives the personality that is our self. All that is "us" lives here in what Lewis called the chest, the seat of magnanimity or greatness. Primarily, this is our will, our emotions, and the source of the three loves called *storge*, *philia*, and *eros*.

Storge is human love experienced by a mother nursing her baby or a father wrestling playfully on the floor with a young son. It is affectionate love.

Philia is the non-physical love between friends and is the most spiritual of the three. While *storge* usually has a biological bond or association, *philia* does not. The affection between friends is not a physical love at all, but rather a bond of mutual agreement.

Friends are friends out of a mutual enjoyment of the other's company.

Eros comprises romantic love. Erotic or sexual affection is part of, though not the same as *eros*. Romantic love often begins with physical attraction, but mature *eros* grows far beyond just that.

Most importantly, all of our actions, i.e., our volitions, come through the heart before they materialize. Volition is our will expressed. All that comes out of us that is good or bad proceeds from the act of our will. The soul is the place of our personality. It is also the seat of a depraved human nature.

Spirit. Our mind, or our spirit, is our head. It is the seat of reason, i.e., our thinking ability. It is where we keep a copy of truth, as we know it. Our reasoning ability considers everything that comes into it against our copy of the truth. The Law of Human Nature lives here too.

Our truth and the real truth may be different. We all jade our copy of truth to some extent in order to benefit ourselves. This is also part of why mankind is utterly depraved. The Law of Human Nature is like a prism through which our copy of truth passes. It compares our truth to real truth, then pokes us with our conscience. If our conscience has become worn and seared, then the pricks and pokes are just dull nudges that we learn to ignore.

Our spirit is where imagination incubates as well. These are imaginations of all things, good or bad, vain or provident.

Breath of God. How did all these parts come to be, and what will happen to them beyond the end of biologic life?

The Bible provides the account of creation, which says that the animals were created before man. No doubt their physical bodies were formed from the earth just as ours. Beyond that though, God does something different. He breathed into man His own breath of life. It does not say he did the same thing with the other animals. This suggests to me that at that same point, God put the spirit and soul, the mind and the heart, into us.

The very breath of God that gives us spirit and soul also breathes into us his Moral Law, The Law of Human Nature. When God finished creating, he made an amazing and very important statement. He proclaimed that everything he created was good. This was his stamp of authenticity, the mark of his very hand on mankind. At this point, there was nothing spoiled in all the natural creation. Mankind contained no hint of depravity.

The Seven Deadly Sins. Dorothy Sayers is well known for her treatise on *The Other Six Deadly Sins*[1], as well as her translation and commentary on all the deadly sins in the Penguin edition of Dante's *Divine Comedy*.[2]

There are seven foundational deadly sins. Like agape love, pride is foundational. Just as all the other characteristics of God are founded on agape love, all the other deadly sins spring out of pride.

The Seven Deadly Sins
1. Pride
2. Envy
3. Wrath
4. Sloth
5. Covetousness
6. Gluttony
7. Lust

Envy is the perverted desire for our own good, which motivates us to deprive others of their good. The focus of envy is not simply an object. It is generalized disdain for all that is good in someone else. Covetousness and avarice, though similar, are not the same as envy. Covetousness is the pervasive desire for something that someone else has, while avarice is the love of money and power.

Wrath is a perverted love of justice that causes one to pursue spiteful revenge. God's wrath however, is not a perversion because it is the settled opposition of his holy nature to all that is evil.[3] His wrath never comes out of any desire to get even. Our wrath is self-serving vengeance, while his wrath is the absolute and perfect measure of perfect justice. The source of his wrath is not out of an emotional response like ours.

Sloth is indifference, i.e., the failure to love any good object. It rises further than simple laziness. It is the conscious indifference to God's will. It is a man's inner voice which says to God, "Whatever!"

Gluttony, for most people, is often associated with food, but it is really far worse. It is the perverted love of pleasure. Lest we think ourselves immune from this, consider all the things that we enjoy in our life. If we have deep-seated cravings for anything that steers our actions like the rudder of a ship, then we have a perverted desire for pleasure.

Lust is the perverted love of persons. Interestingly, this is not just limited to *eros* or erotic love. Lust can also be present within *storge* and *philia*. Lewis gives a quite common example of lust within *storge* in *The Great Divorce*[4] and idolatrous lust can occur within the marriage relationship, unfortunately.[5]

Four Cardinal Virtues. There are four cardinal virtues, and they are pivotal. The original Latin word for cardinal means "the hinge of a door." Cardinal virtues have throughout time been recognized across multiple cultures and all civilized people, as well.

> The Four Cardinal Virtues
> 1. Wisdom
> 2. Moderation or Temperance
> 3. Courage
> 4. Justice or Keeping Promises

The Lord Jesus Christ's very words in Matthew 5:3–13 tell us what the hallmarks of a whole man are. This is a section of Scripture known as the Beatitudes. We tend to scan over these quickly when reading them, but we should recognize that many of these are direct opposites of the seven deadly sins. They are very important measures to size ourselves up.

3 ¶ Blessed are the poor in spirit: for theirs is the kingdom of heaven.

4 Blessed are they that mourn: for they shall be comforted.

5 Blessed are the meek: for they shall inherit the earth.

6 Blessed are they which do hunger and thirst after righteousness: for they shall be filled.

7 Blessed are the merciful: for they shall obtain mercy.

8 Blessed are the pure in heart: for they shall see God.

9 Blessed are the peacemakers: for they shall be called the children of God.

10 Blessed are they which are persecuted for righteousness' sake: for theirs is the kingdom of heaven.

11 Blessed are ye, when men shall revile you, and persecute you, and shall say all manner of evil against you falsely, for my sake. 12 ejoice, and be exceeding glad: for great is your reward in heaven: for so persecuted they the prophets which were before you.

13 ¶ Ye are the salt of the earth: but if the salt have lost his savour, wherewith shall it be salted? it is thenceforth good for nothing, but to be cast out, and to be trodden under foot of men. (Matt. 5:3–13 KJV)

Wisdom occurs when our reason apprehends truth and then governs our will. Our heart receives wisdom, and then our volition acts accordingly. This results in courage, justice, goodwill, a pure heart, and compassion. Moderation occurs when our heart then overrules any fleshly desires or impulses.

Courage is the testing point of all the other virtues. Justice is the evidence and results of courage. Chivalry is the combination of courage and justice with the personality trait of gentleness.

How we reason is terribly important, as Proverbs 23:7 clearly states.

> 7 For as he thinketh in his heart, so is he: Eat and drink, saith he to thee; but his heart is not with thee. (Prov. 23:7 KJV))

When our reason, i.e., our intellect, becomes dark or downcast, we cannot apprehend truth. Our will and volition produce cowardice, injustice, envy, sloth, or wrath. Attacks on the mind are specifically intended to darken the intellect for this very reason.[6] The effect cascades dramatically and disastrously as 2 Corinthians 4:4 shows.

> 4 In whom the god of this world hath blinded the minds of them which believe not, lest the light of the glorious gospel of Christ, who is the image of God, should shine unto them.(2 Cor. 4:4 KJV)

Vain imaginations directly affect both truth and reason, which also serves to darken the intellect as described in Romans 1:21. This darkening can affect the Heart as well.

> 1 ¶ I beseech you therefore, brethren, by the mercies of God, that ye present your bodies a living sacrifice, holy, acceptable unto God, which is your reasonable service. (Rom. 12:1 KJV)

Now you might have wondered why I show volition in its own compartment. All sin that comes out of our volition leaves black marks on our soul. Once a black mark is present, we cannot erase or cover it. The process of interaction between reason, truth, and will occurs instantly and there is certainly interaction. What happens when we think bad thoughts? Do they instantly become these black marks? Mark 7:15 is quite clear here.

> 15 There is nothing from without a man, that entering into him can defile him: but the things which come out of him, those are they that defile the man. (Mark 7:15 KJV)

Thoughts constantly flow into our reason and we instantly reference it against truth. At that moment, we have the opportunity to discard it. If we don't discard it, we can deposit it into our imagination, where we may revisit it, even repeatedly obsess on it time after time. If it is a vain imagination and we revisit it, we can alter our copy of truth. Folly and foolishness rather than wisdom is then injected into our will. In our heart, the vain imagination becomes an act of our volition and produces sin, a black mark on our soul.

It is critical that we actively take every thought captive as stated in 2 Corinthians 10:5. Even more, though, we actively need to nurture good thoughts according to Philippians 4:8.

> 5 Casting down imaginations, and every high thing that exalteth itself against the knowledge of God, and bringing into captivity every thought to the obedience of Christ; (2 Cor. 10:5 KJV)

> ⁸ Finally, brethren, whatsoever things are true, whatsoever things are honest, whatsoever things are just, whatsoever things are pure, whatsoever things are lovely, whatsoever things are of good report; if there be any virtue, and if there be any praise, think on these things. (Phil. 4:8 KJV)

When reason apprehends truth, the will governs and overrules the belly. Moderation, i.e., temperance, must constantly throttle the impulses and desires of our flesh. It is important to understand that desires for food, sex, etc., have a legitimate presence in our flesh. Remember when God created man, he said it was good. He has provided a way for those desires to be met in a legitimate way, but he never intended us to be ruled by the belly.

Controlling desires of the flesh starts in the spirit. We must take every thought captive so we can moderate the flesh, otherwise covetousness, gluttony, or lust results. However, sometimes certain of these desires must be encouraged and fanned, such as in the marriage bed. A husband and a wife have a duty to encourage and nurture healthy sexual impulses toward each other, since marriage of the two is culminated in that physical connection. Paul is very clear in 1 Corinthians 7:1–9.

> ¹ Now concerning the things whereof ye wrote unto me: It is good for a man not to touch a woman. ² Nevertheless, to avoid fornication, let every man have his own wife, and let every woman have her own husband. ³ Let the husband render unto the wife due

benevolence: and likewise also the wife unto the husband. 4 The wife hath not power of her own body, but the husband: and likewise also the husband hath not power of his own body, but the wife. 5 Defraud ye not one the other, except it be with consent for a time, that ye may give yourselves to fasting and prayer; and come together again, that Satan tempt you not for your incontinency. 6 But I speak this by permission, and not of commandment. 7 For I would that all men were even as I myself. But every man hath his proper gift of God, one after this manner, and another after that. 8 I say therefore to the unmarried and widows, It is good for them if they abide even as I. 9 But if they cannot contain, let them marry: for it is better to marry than to burn. (1 Cor. 7:1-9 KJV)

All the cardinal virtues and the deadly sins have a presence within and expression outside of us. What we say and do that results in a volitional expression of any sin leaves a black mark on our soul. It is that black mark that cannot be erased, even when the offended person has granted forgiveness. Our words echo in testimony against us forever.

But there is another black mark whose presence is not caused by any volitional act. It is the black mark of human depravity. The black marks of our individual selves prove its existence. We are utterly fallen creatures, seduced and captured by temptation in the first place. We suffer from a sinful nature which is the source of our depravity and from sin we commit.

We could perhaps decide to continually do better until we come to a place where we can control most all the volitional sins. But what do we do about the black marks we have already accumulated? And what about the black mark of our human depravity? We can never fix that ourselves.

Guide To Kohlenberger/ Mounce Hebrew-Aramaic Dictionary

Throughout this book you will see references to Hebrew words from which are translated the English word we read. Translation simply refers to interpreting and translating texts written from one language into another. The Old Testament is translated from original Hebrew while the New Testament comes from Greek. Sometimes there are translations of translation. That is beyond the scope of this reference source.

Here is an example Kohlenberger/Mounce reference. The word "take" in Exodus 12:3 is translated this way in the Hebrew dictionary. Take note how it carries the sense of marriage.

> **GK H4374 | S H3947** לָקַח *lāqaḥ* 967x v. [root of: 4375, 4376, 4917, 4918?, 4920, 5228, 5229]. **Q** to take, receive; **Qp** to be led away; **N** to be captured, taken away; **Pu** to be taken away, brought; **Ht** to flash back and forth; by extension: to gain possession, exercise authority; "to take a woman" means "to marry a

wife". » accept; capture; choose; deprive; get; grasp; marry; receive; seize; take.

It starts with the reference ids of the word. The first here is GK H4374. The "GK" refers to the Goodrick-Kohlenberger number. The second id is the Strong's number and is indicated by the "S." In both cases the "H" refers to the source text being Hebrew. The Strong's Dictionary also has phonetic pronunciations.

Following the reference ids is the Hebrew source word itself and the English pronunciation key. In this reference, the word לָקַח (lāqah, law-kakh´)is found 967 times in the Hebrew Old Testament. Next it is identified as a verb by the small "v" and other root words are given by their Kohlenberger/Mounce id number.

Following that are the various English translations for לָקַח (lāqah, law-kakh´) each which is preceded by a bold letter. Each bold letter indicates the translation for a particular tense of the Hebrew word. Without knowing a little about Hebrew, it is difficult to identify what tense a particular word is. Suffice it to say that the way a particular translated word is interpreted in the English we see in the Old Testament is dependent on that tense and the expertise of the translator who is doing the translation.

Because translation is dependent on the varied expertise of the translator and focus of the translation, we have the different versions of the Holy Bible. Each translator is expressing the English the way he understands it. Usually there are teams of translators so that we get the best English word from their consensus opinion. The King James Bible was originally translated by a combined group containing two subgroups of opposing scholars. This is why the King James version was a marvel of scholarly thought when it was created.

But English now is notably different from the English of King James's day. Old English is even more disparate from today's English. This is not just based on the meaning of specific words, however, but also on the varied interpretations of those words all within English speakers of the same time period.

The Living Bible was a translation to natural spoken language and was an attempt to make the Bible more accessible and understandable to the person with an average eduction. Other translations have come along since, each with a prescribed focus based on current English language use. You will find that most of the translations I use quote the English Standard Version of the Holy Bible. This does not mean that everyone has to use that version. I personally like and use it because it seems to give me a more accurate flavor of the original text. That is not always the case. Look at the difference between the Amplified and English Standard Version of the same verse in Psalms.

> [10] Mercy and loving-kindness and truth have met together; righteousness and peace have kissed each other. (Ps. 85:10 AMP)

> [10] Mercy and truth are met together; righteousness and peace have kissed each other.(Ps. 85:10 KJV)

The Amplified version is where the phrase "mercy kisses justice" comes from, but the English Standard Version does not use the word "mercy" at all. Both these versions are helpful though because they increase my understanding and show how that phrase comes to be.

Though this is not intended to be a primer in any way, here is the partial list of Kohlenberger/Mounce keys showing example Hebrew verb tense comparisons[1]

Abbreviation	Full Form	Mood	Voice	Example
Q	Qal or Paal	Simple	Active	He cut
Qp	Qal passive	Simple	Passive	He is cut
N	Niphal	Simple	Passive	He was cut
P	Piel	Intensive	Active	He slashed
Pu	Paul	Intensive	Passive	He was slashed
H	Hiphil	Causative	Active	He made cut
Ho	Hophal	Causative	Passive	He was made cut
Hi	Hithpael	Intensive	Reflexive	He slashed himself

Bibliography & Endnotes

Alghieri, Dante. *The Comedy of Dante Alighieri, the Florentine: The Divine Comedy 1, 2, 3*. Translated by Dorothy L. Sayers. New York: Penguin Books, 1949.

Chamblin, Knox. *C. S. Lewis - Dr. Knox Chamblin*. Podcast. Reformed Theological Seminary, 1998. Podcast, https://itunes.apple.com/us/course/c.s.-lewis/id556900693.

Kohlenberger, John R., and James A. Swanson. *The Hebrew English Concordance to the Old Testament*. Zondervan, 1998.

Lewis, C. S. *The Great Divorce*. ePub. New York: Harper One, 2009. ePub, https://itun.es/us/aMVFv.l.

Lewis, C. S. *Mere Christianity*. New York: Harper Collins, 2009. https://books.apple.com/us/book/mere-christianity/id360638379

Lewis, C. S. *The Problem of Pain*. ePub. New York: Harper One, 2009. ePub, https://books.apple.com/us/book/mere-christianity/id360638379.

Lewis, C. S. *The Screwtape Letters (Enhanced Special Edition)*. ePub. New York: Harper One, 2009. ePub, https://itun.es/us/Pckuz.l.

Mounce, William D., and Rick D. Bennett, eds. *Mounce Concise Greek-English Dictionary of the New Testament*. Altamonte Springs, FL: Oak Tree, 2011.

Neilson, William Allan, Thomas Albert Knott, and Paul Worthington Carhart. *Webster's New International Dictionary of the English Language. 2d Ed., Unabridged: An Entirely New Book Utilizing All the Experience and Resources of More Than One Hundred Years of Genuine Webster Dictionaries*. 1941.

Pink, A. W. *Objections to God's Sovereignty Answered*. 1990.

Sayers, Dorothy Leigh. *The Other Six Deadly Sins, an Address Given to the Public Morality Council At Caxton Hall,*

Scofield, Cyrus I., and Doris W. Rikkers, eds. *The Scofield® Study Bible Notes*. Oxford, England: Oxford University Press, 2003.

Vanauken, Sheldon. *A Severe Mercy*. ePub. New York: Harper One, 2011. ePub, https://itun.es/us/WY9tA.l.

Walls, Jerry *What's Wrong With Calvinism, Part 1*. Video. *https://www.youtube.com/watch?v=Daomzm3nyIg*

Chapter One

[1] Cyrus I. Scofield, and Doris W. Rikkers, eds. *The Scofield® Study Bible Notes*.

Chapter Two

[1] Mounce, William D. and Rick D. Bennett, Jr., *Mounce Concise Greek-English Dictionary of the New Testament*, William D. Mounce, ©2011.

[2] Kohlenberger, John R., III and Mounce, William D., *Kohlenberger/Mounce Concise Hebrew-Aramaic English Dictionary of the Old Testament*, William D. Mounce, ©2012.

[3] Ibid., *Kohlenberger/Mounce Concise Hebrew-Aramaic English Dictionary of the Old Testament*.

[4] Ibid. *Mounce Concise Greek-English Dictionary of the New Testament*.

[5] Ibid. *Mounce Concise Greek-English Dictionary of the New Testament*.

[6] Ibid. *Mounce Concise Greek-English Dictionary of the New Testament*.

Chapter Three

[1] Mounce, William D. and Rick D. Bennett, Jr., *Mounce Concise Greek-English Dictionary of the New Testament*, William D. Mounce, ©2011.

[2] Kohlenberger, John R., III and Mounce, William D., *Kohlenberger/Mounce Concise Hebrew-Aramaic English Dictionary of the Old Testament*, William D. Mounce, ©2012.

[3] Ibid., *Kohlenberger/Mounce Concise Hebrew-Aramaic English Dictionary of the Old Testament*.

[4] Ibid., *Kohlenberger/Mounce Concise Hebrew-Aramaic English Dictionary of the Old Testament*.

[5] Ibid., *Kohlenberger/Mounce Concise Hebrew-Aramaic English Dictionary of the Old Testament*.

Chapter Four

[1] Kohlenberger, John R., III and Mounce, William D., *Kohlenberger/Mounce Concise Hebrew-Aramaic English Dictionary of the Old Testament*, William D. Mounce, ©2012.

[2] Ibid., *Kohlenberger/Mounce Concise Hebrew-Aramaic English Dictionary of the Old Testament*.

[3] Ibid., *Kohlenberger/Mounce Concise Hebrew-Aramaic English Dictionary of the Old Testament*.

[4] Mounce, William D. and Rick D. Bennett, Jr., *Mounce Concise Greek-English Dictionary of the New Testament*, William D. Mounce, ©2011.

[5] Ibid. *Mounce Concise Greek-English Dictionary of the New Testament.*

[6] Ibid. *Mounce Concise Greek-English Dictionary of the New Testament.*

Chapter Five

[1] Mounce, William D. and Rick D. Bennett, Jr., *Mounce Concise Greek-English Dictionary of the New Testament*, William D. Mounce, ©2011.

[2] Ibid. *Mounce Concise Greek-English Dictionary of the New Testament.*

[3] Ibid. *Mounce Concise Greek-English Dictionary of the New Testament.*

Chapter Six

[1] Lewis, C. S. *Mere Christianity.* New York: Harper Collins, 2009. https://books.apple.com/us/book/mere-christianity/id360638379

[2] Time Dilation Table, ©2020 Ron Smith, MD, reprinted from *Between Justice and Mercy with Related Essays.*

Chapter Seven

[1] Kohlenberger, John R., III and Mounce, William D., *Kohlenberger/Mounce Concise Hebrew-Aramaic English Dictionary of the Old Testament*, William D. Mounce, ©2012.

[2] Mounce, William D. and Rick D. Bennett, Jr., *Mounce Concise Greek-English Dictionary of the New Testament*, William D. Mounce, ©2011.

[3] Ibid. *Mounce Concise Greek-English Dictionary of the New Testament.*

[4] Ibid., *Kohlenberger/Mounce Concise Hebrew-Aramaic English Dictionary of the Old Testament.*

[5] Ibid., *Kohlenberger/Mounce Concise Hebrew-Aramaic English Dictionary of the Old Testament.*

[6] Ibid., *Kohlenberger/Mounce Concise Hebrew-Aramaic English Dictionary of the Old Testament.*

[7] Ibid., *Kohlenberger/Mounce Concise Hebrew-Aramaic English Dictionary of the Old Testament.*

[8] Ibid., *Kohlenberger/Mounce Concise Hebrew-Aramaic English Dictionary of the Old Testament.*

[9] Ibid. *Mounce Concise Greek-English Dictionary of the New Testament.*

[10] Pink, A. W. *Objections to God's Sovereignty Answered*

[11] Walls, Jerry *What's Wrong With Calvinism, Part 1.*

Chapter Eight

[1] Kohlenberger, John R., III and Mounce, William D., *Kohlenberger/Mounce Concise Hebrew-Aramaic English Dictionary of the Old Testament*, William D. Mounce, ©2012.

[2] Ibid., *Kohlenberger/Mounce Concise Hebrew-Aramaic English Dictionary of the Old Testament.*

[3] Ibid., *Kohlenberger/Mounce Concise Hebrew-Aramaic English Dictionary of the Old Testament.*

[4] Ibid., *Kohlenberger/Mounce Concise Hebrew-Aramaic English Dictionary of the Old Testament.*

[5] See Psalm 16:8-11.

[6] See Jeremiah 31:34, Hebrews 8:12, Hebrews 10:17, and Psalm 103:12.

Chapter Nine

[1] Lewis, C. S. *Mere Christianity.*

[2] Neilson, W. A. Knott, T. A., and Carhart, P. W. *Webster's New International Dictionary of the English Language. 2d Ed., Unabridged: An Entirely New Book Utilizing All the Experience and Resources of More Than One Hundred Years of Genuine Webster Dictionaries*, p. 1819

Laura's Story

[1] Lewis, C. S. *Mere Christianity.*

Our Spiritual Anatomy

[1] Dorothy Sayers, *The Other Six Deadly Sins: An Address Given to the Public Morality Council at Caxton Hall, Westminster, on October 23rd, 1941.*

[2] Alighieri Dante, *The Divine Comedy* [in Italian] trans. by Dorothy L. Sayers.

[3] Knox Chamblin, "C. S. Lewis. - Dr. Knox Chamblin" iTunes U, 1998, https://itunes.apple.com/us/course/c.s.-lewis/id556900693.

[4] C. S. Lewis, *The Great Divorce.*

[5] Sheldon Vanauken, *A Severe Mercy.*

[6] C. S. Lewis, *The Screwtape Letters.*

Guide To Kohlenberger/Mounce Hebrew-Aramaic Dictionary

[1] Benner, Jeff A., Ancient Hebrew Reference Center, https://www.ancient-hebrew.org/roots-words/about-hebrew-nouns-and-verbs.htm

Milton Keynes UK
Ingram Content Group UK Ltd.
UKHW012313040624
443649UK00007B/611